A Beginner's Guide to Discourse Analysis

A Beginner's Guide to Discourse Analysis

Sean Sutherland

University of Westminster, UK

 macmillan
international
HIGHER EDUCATION

 RED GLOBE
PRESS

First published 2016 by
RED GLOBE PRESS

Red Globe Press in the UK is an imprint of Springer Nature Limited,
registered in England, company number 785998, of 4 Crinan Street,
London, N1 9XW.

Red Globe Press® is a registered trademark in the United States,
the United Kingdom, Europe and other countries.

ISBN 978–1–137–40288–2   ISBN 978–1–137–40289–9 (eBook)

This book is printed on paper suitable for recycling and made from fully
managed and sustained forest sources. Logging, pulping and manufacturing
processes are expected to conform to the environmental regulations
of the country of origin.

A catalogue record for this book is available from the British Library.

A catalog record for this book is available from the Library of Congress.

Contents

Acknowledgements

Thank you to my colleagues at the University of Westminster for their professional guidance and assistance over the years. I would especially like to thank Dr Charles Denroche for providing me with some ideas that led to the development of the classes on which much of this book is based. Thank you also to my wife Gwen and daughter Macie for their continuing support.

The authors and publisher wish to thank the following for permission to reproduce copyright material:

- *The Daily Mash* for the article "London Property Market Based on People Pretending Grim Places are Great," in Chapter 4
- Ellena Ashley for an excerpt from the fairy tale *The Dragon Rock*, in Chapter 5
- Bansri Kakkad for the spoken data extract recorded and transcribed, in Chapter 5.

Introduction

Think about the sentence "I'm hungry." If I'm at home with my young daughter and she says "I'm hungry", anyone listening would have a feeling that she means "Feed me" or "Give me some food." I have a responsibility to care for my daughter, that care involves making sure she is fed, and she's not old enough to feed herself, so when I hear the words "I'm hungry", I take them as meaning something different to what she says. If I was only focused on the words, not the meaning, I might hear "I'm hungry" and respond with "I'm tired", guessing that we were talking about our physical states. (Or I might say, "Pleased to meet you, Hungry. I'm Sean", a silly joke that kids seem to like.) However, in reality I react to what my daughter means, not to what she says, and take the appropriate action by finding her something to eat.

If I'm out with a friend and he says "I'm hungry", which are the same words, they mean something different. If I've just asked him what he wants to do, his words might now mean "Let's eat." My relationship with my friends is different from my relationship with my daughter. I don't have the same responsibility to feed my friends, unless I have invited them to dinner, so hearing "I'm hungry" might be seen as an offer to eat together. If a student in my class says "I'm hungry", I would probably arrive at a different understanding of what she means. I don't have any responsibility to feed my students. I don't eat with them except on rare occasions such as after graduation, and never in the classroom. I might then understand that the student is giving an excuse, explaining that she wants to leave the classroom to buy a snack.

To really understand language we can't just look at the words, although they are of course important. We have to think about who (my daughter, a friend, a student) is talking to whom (a father, a friend, a lecturer), where (at home, a public place, a classroom) and for what purpose (a demand for food, an offer to eat, an excuse for leaving).

Text, in linguistic terms, means "the words used in a language event". Texts include speeches by one person, conversations that include many speakers (all the participants' words count as part of the text), songs, novels, restaurant menus, newspaper articles and so on.

Discourse, as many linguists use the term, means the text, that is, the language used, plus the context in which it appears. "I'm hungry" is only properly understood by thinking about the words and who said them to whom in what place. "I'm hungry" is a bit of discourse that could mean a variety of things, depending on the context. In this book I use the terms *text* and *discourse* as they are appropriate, but it is often difficult to discuss texts without considering them as part of discourse, so the terms are sometimes interchangeable. Words are always used in a certain context.

Discourse analysis means "the study of language in use". Language can be analysed without thinking about the context, for instance if we said that "I'm hungry" is a subject, a verb and an adjective. *To do discourse analysis* means that we must take account of those individual words of the text, but we must also recognise that people use language in many different contexts, and understanding those contexts is necessary if we want to understand language.

Discourse analysis can be done to either spoken language or written language. Some authors make a distinction between "spoken discourse" and "written texts" (Jackson & Stockwell, 2011), but I don't think this is always a useful distinction. Whether someone says "I'm hungry" or sends me a text message saying the same thing, I have to understand that message based on thinking about those words, but also by thinking about who is speaking or writing and what my relationship is with that person.

Let's look at another example of discourse analysis. I often eavesdrop on other people's conversations. This is not entirely because I'm nosey about other people's lives, although I am, but rather it is because I like hearing how different people talk. I'm mostly interested in the different ways that people can say things, not so much in what they are actually talking about.

When I first began teaching at a British university, I had many chances to hear people using language in ways that were new to me. I'm not British and I was in my late thirties when I started lecturing in London, so hearing young people from Britain and the rest of the world speaking all around me throughout the day kept me very busy eavesdropping. It was fascinating then, and remains so now, to hear how differently they could use language when compared to me and to one another, despite the fact that we were all speaking English.

I still clearly recall a striking example of language use that caught my attention and set me to thinking about the topics which are discussed in this book. I saw Kiran, a student at the university, approach another young woman named Rana who had a mobile phone in her hand. Kiran looked at Rana and her phone, then said, "You got an iPhone, you cow."

The first part of this utterance, "You got an iPhone", is interesting enough. (Note that I'm using **utterance** here to mean "small amount of spoken language", without worrying about whether it is a word, phrase, clause or sentence.) Why would Kiran point out something so obvious? Certainly Rana knew that she had a phone. But leave that aside for a moment and look at the second part: "you cow". I know a cow is a farm animal; Rana was obviously not one. I also know that *cow* can be used as a slur to insult people, relying on some common perceptions we have of cows as large, lazy and unintelligent. However, Rana's reaction did not show her to be insulted. She laughed and explained that her family had recently signed up for a phone plan which included new phones. Kiran explained that she had wanted to get one but could not afford to do so. The two women spoke for a few more minutes, then walked off discussing where they would go for lunch.

It appeared that *cow* here was not insulting. Instead, Kiran appears to have used it to show that she was jealous of Rana, that she thought Rana was lucky to have such a phone, and that she was happy for Rana. Kiran could rely on her existing relationship with Rana, one that was quite obviously friendly, to help Rana interpret "you cow" as something other than an insult. Within the context of their relationship "you cow" was interpreted as something quite opposed to an insult. It was a signal that their relationship was of a type in which cow could not possibly be interpreted as an insult and so had to be taken as a sign of affection. Here "cow" had a social meaning, akin to saying "We're friends."

This is discourse analysis. Individual words, phrases and clauses have meaning on their own, but they can only be understood by looking at their **co-text**, the words that surround them, and at their **context**, the real-world situations in which the words are used. Cow sometimes means "farm animal", sometimes is an insult and sometimes means "We're friends".

In Lewis Carroll's *Alice in Wonderland*, Humpty Dumpty says, "When I use a word... it means just what I choose it to mean – neither more nor less." Alice is unconvinced, asking if people can use words to mean more than one thing. Humpty Dumpty replies, "The question is which is to be master – that's all." Discourse analysts, and linguists in general, agree with Mr Dumpty. Words mean what people want them to mean. It doesn't matter that the dictionary might not list "We're friends" as a meaning of *cow*. A discourse analytic look at Kiran and Rana's exchange makes it clear that they agreed that it meant that.

If you're interested in language, I suggest you eavesdrop, talk and listen, and read as much as you possibly can. The world is full of language in use, so the discourses waiting to be analysed are innumerable. You'll never be bored at even the most terrible film if you focus on the language and ignore the cardboard actors, boring plot and unfunny jokes. Think about why the characters talk as they do and compare their discourse to what you know about how real people talk.

The rest of this book is an explanation of some of the things that linguists think about when they analyse discourse. In **Chapter 1** we look at texts, including those features that allow us to see how different parts of a text are joined together into a cohesive unit larger than any one word or sentence within it. In **Chapter 2** we begin to look at discourse by examining how we make meaning from texts in which not everything that is meant is actually spoken aloud or written down. In **Chapter 3** we examine the producers (writers and speakers) of discourse, thinking about ways that they differ from each other and how that affects the discourses that they produce. In **Chapter 4** we discuss how the context of discourse helps shape the linguistic features that appear within it. In **Chapter 5** we look at the information presented in discourse: how it is organised, how certain parts can be highlighted, and how some parts of the information can be omitted, yet understood by those who read or listen.

Chapter 1

Thinking about the Text

In this chapter we look at the relations between words that make up discourse, specifically the links between words that join them into what linguists call a *text*. We then examine some features of spoken conversations, a genre of text that is of particular interest to discourse analysts because of its high frequency in daily life and its special function as a means of creating and maintaining social relations.

Look at the letters *abc* in that order. You'll probably think of them as the first three letters of the alphabet. One of the first songs many children learn is the alphabet song, so people will often think of the alphabet when they see *abc*.

Now look at the letters in the order *cab*. You'll now recognise them as a word. As a regular user of English, you know a surprising number of words. At the time you started school you probably knew a few thousand words. By the time you became an adult you knew tens of thousands.

You might not use tens of thousands of words regularly, but you know them when you see them. For example, you probably talk about *going up* a staircase or *climbing* the stairs quite regularly, but I doubt you often say that you *ascend* the stairs, even if you recognise that word. That's the difference between your **productive language skills** (speaking and writing) and your **receptive language skills** (listening and reading). Most of the time when we produce language, we rely on comfortable words that we use often. When we receive language, we're able to understand many more words, even if we rarely use them ourselves.

You might not be an English teacher or a linguist, but you certainly have a lot of tools in your head for determining what is acceptable in English and what is not. Returning to our three letters, what if

1

they were in the order *bac*? A doctor or nurse might think of *bac* as the initialism for "blood alcohol content", but that should be written *BAC*, as **initialisms** are usually written in capital letters. Although you realise that *bac* is not a word on its own, you will quickly see that it could be part of a word such as *back*, *tobacco* or even *antibacterial* if you add more letters.

Now consider the letters in the order *acb*. That doesn't look like a possible pattern for letters in an English word, even if we add more letters. Your spelling tool, the accumulation of knowledge you have that tells you what works and what doesn't work in English, probably can't do anything with the combination *acb*. As a regular user of English, you're pretty good at recognising which patterns of letters are allowed and which patterns are not.

Note that we are looking at written words here, but if we were talking to each other in person about this, you could think the same way about the possible sound combinations of English. Some sound patterns are possible, some are not and some only occur at times. (This is the study of **phonology**, the sound system of languages.) For example, we don't usually start words with a *t* sound followed by an *s* sound in English. When pronouncing a word like *tsunami* that English borrowed from Japanese, some people won't be sure whether we should try to pronounce the *t* or not. Is it pronounced *tsu-na-mi* or *su-na-mi*? There isn't really a correct answer to this. It depends on whether you want to pronounce the word like a Japanese person would, or in a way that sounds English. (Most English speakers don't have a problem pronouncing a *ts* sound at the end of words, of course. Think of *rabbits* and *habits*.)

When you think about how letters are organised through spelling rules into written words or about how sounds are organised through phonological rules into spoken words, you're taking advantage of one of the tools you have in your head for analysing language. When you looked at *acb* and decided that it was not part of an English word, you were drawing on your knowledge of spelling, your spelling tool, to analyse that letter combination.

You have another tool at your disposal to help you think about how language works. It tells you how the words that you know are organised into acceptable patterns. This tool is called *grammar*. *Grammar* is an odd word. Some people grow up learning English, they speak it regularly, they hear it on TV and radio, they write emails and text messages and they read English books, magazines and newspapers. They use grammar to recognise acceptable patterns of words constantly, yet they regularly say things like "I'm really bad at English grammar." What they mean, I think, is that they can't explain grammar: they don't remember the difference between active and passive voice, they can't recall what a gerund is and so on. Of course they are good at using grammar. If they weren't, they wouldn't be able to say or write anything that made sense.

When you read or hear "He ate the apple", you know that it is grammatically acceptable. It makes sense. You're relying on some of the rules of grammar that you know to analyse those four words and decide that together they make up an acceptable English sentence. If you see "The apple he ate", you probably get a feeling that those words are possible in that order but more words are needed to make it complete. "The apple he ate was delicious" is one way you could turn those four words into a complete sentence. What about "Ate apple the he?" I don't think you can do anything to make that into a sentence. Those are four words that are not organised properly. Just as you knew that *cab* was a possible pattern of letters but *acb* wasn't, your knowledge of grammar tells you which patterns of words are possible and which are not.

This chapter is not about spelling, phonology or grammar. It is about words and sentences, either written or spoken, that are important **linguistic units** to consider when we discuss the organisation of language. Sounds are organised into words through phonological rules, and words are organised into sentences through grammatical rules. For many people, their education about the various linguistic units stopped at that point, but linguists often talk about the next level of linguistic unit, one bigger than words and sentences. They call this next level a **text**.

People use *text* to mean a variety of things: a text message, a textbook, and words on a computer screen could each be called *text*. That's fine. People use words to mean different things depending on what they are talking about. Linguists know those definitions of *text*, but they also use the word *text* as a convenient way of referring to *all* kinds of different types of language. Linguists use *text* to mean "a set of coherent words that present a message". All of the words in the text work together, that is, they are **coherent**, to create a message bigger than any one word on its own. This means that things we might normally think of as texts, such as textbooks, novels and Shakespeare's plays, *are* texts, but so are things that might not be immediately obvious, such as recipes, bus schedules, songs, newspaper articles and instruction manuals.

Sometimes people seem shy about using the word *text* to refer to these everyday things. They recall their school teachers calling great works of literature *texts*, so it may seem that calling a recipe for chicken soup a text is a bit silly. It's common to feel a bit odd using words in new ways. I've heard people say they don't like ordering coffee from Starbucks because they are expected to say *short* and *tall* instead of *small* and *large*. (Or is a *tall* a medium and a *grande* a large?) We're comfortable using words that we know because we know precisely how to use them. You might feel like you were being pompous if you were to use the phrase *acute myocardial infarction* instead of the common one *heart attack*.

Linguists are not calling things *texts* to be pompous. They use the word because it is a convenient way to refer to things that have some elements in common, although they may be quite different in other ways.

Cohesion

Returning to the chicken soup I mentioned earlier, how can long, complex novels have something in common with a short, simple recipe for a hot lunch? The first thing to consider when looking at what defines a text is to think about how the words in the text are connected to each other in a way that makes it clear that they belong together. Halliday and Hasan (1976), in their influential book *Cohesion in English*, explain that **cohesion** is the collective name for all of those links that connect the different parts of a text. Look at the following sentence:

1.1
We showed it to him yesterday, but he forgot.

You certainly understand all of the words in that sentence. You know that it means roughly "More than one person showed something to one person yesterday, but the person who was showed forgot." More specifically, you know that *him*, for example, refers to a single male being, probably a human, but maybe an animal or alien. You know how *him* works, but you don't actually know who *him* is here, do you? *Him* is a form of **reference**, a word that has some meaning on its own, but has a more specific meaning if we refer somewhere else in the text. *Him* refers to someone, but we don't know who he is. This is the difference between a word that you understand and a word that is interpretable. A word that is **interpretable** is a word that refers specifically to someone or something. *Him* in 1.1 is **uninterpretable** because you know the word's usual function, but you don't know what it really means. If we add another sentence, you'll see that you know more about *him*.

1.2
Vikram said he hadn't seen the book before. We showed it to him yesterday, but he forgot.

Now you can see what *him* means very specifically. *Him* refers to *Vikram*. In 1.2 *him* is interpretable, as we know that it refers to *Vikram* and only *Vikram*. It doesn't refer to any other person in this text, although of course in other texts, *him* would refer to someone else. Halliday and Hasan explained this property of *him* and similar words by saying that these words **presuppose** something else. When we see these words, we know how they work, but we also know that we need more information to interpret them. In 1.2 you had to look back in the text to interpret *him*. This is called **anaphoric reference**. This process of looking back applies to either looking back through the printed words of a written text or to looking back in time through the words of a spoken text.

Those things that are being referred back to can be called either **referents** or **antecedents**. In the previous example the reference *him* refers to the referent *Vikram*. The words *reference* and *referent* complement each other nicely in form, but sometimes when we talk, they can be confusing as *reference* sounds like the plural form *referents*. I've often been asked, "Did you say *reference* or *referents*?", so I tend to say *antecedent*.

It is also possible to refer forward to words that will come later in the text. This is called **cataphoric reference**. When someone says,

"Listen to this", the word *this* is uninterpretable. You don't know what it means until the person continues to talk. Using cataphoric reference is a way of engaging someone in the text. Saying "Listen to this", might signal that the speaker is about to tell a new joke, explain something important or deliver some exciting news.

Toni Morrison's novel *Paradise* starts with the sentence "They shoot the white girl first", which is an excellent example of how cataphoric reference can draw readers into a story. Those six words create several questions in readers' minds. Who are *they*? Who is *the* white girl? (*The* is also a reference, as it points at a specific person here, but we don't know who she is yet.) Why was she shot?

Anaphoric reference and cataphoric reference are known together as **endophoric reference**, which means that they refer to words that are found in the text. The other words in the text can be called the co-text, so an endophoric reference refers to something in the co-text, the words that the reference appears with.

There are also references that refer to things outside of the text. When someone says, "Look at that" and points, we don't know what *that* is from the person's words, we will only know from looking at whatever is being pointed at. This is known as **exophoric reference**. An exophoric reference refers to the **context**, which is the physical space or situation in which the text is produced. (Think of the *en* in *endophoric* as meaning *in* the text and the *exo* in *exophoric* as meaning *exit* or *out* of the text. That's how I remember them.) When you're talking to someone in person, it is often convenient to use exophoric references to the context in which you're talking because you can both see the same things ("Do you want *this*?") and hear the same things ("What was *that* noise?"). When an author writes a book, he or she doesn't usually know where someone will read it, so it is difficult to use exophoric references, but there can still be numerous endophoric references to the co-text because the reader can look back and forth through the words.

Look back at 1.2. (Vikram said he hadn't seen the book before. We showed it to him yesterday, but he forgot.) You should now be able to see that *it* in the second sentence is interpretable because *it* is an anaphoric reference, pointing back to *the book*. *We*, on the other hand, is uninterpretable. We don't know who *we* is here. It's more than one person, but we don't know which people. (Note that *we* is also interesting as it can be inclusive or exclusive. **Inclusive** *we* refers to both the speaker and the listener, such as when I say "We should have lunch together sometime", to you. **Exclusive** *we* refers to the speaker and other people, but doesn't include the listener, as in "We'd appreciate it if you'd be quiet for a minute.")

Cohesion, as Halliday and Hasan define it, is like glue that holds the text together. Glue is adhesive, meaning it sticks to other things, but glue is also cohesive, meaning it sticks to itself. In the same way, different parts of a text have to be sticky or cohesive. As you read or listen to a text, you encounter numerous words like *him*, *they* and *it*, which refer anaphorically or cataphorically to other parts of the text. Since you're reading or listening to the whole text, you can interpret these words and see how they help different sections of the text stick together. You can see that the whole text, despite being made up of many words and sentences, belongs together as a linguistic unit.

Someone who comes into the room part-way through a speech or who starts reading a book in the middle will find many of the references uninterpretable. When you pass people on the street, you'll often hear them say things like, "She said so but he didn't think we should use the green one." There are several words in that sentence that presuppose that the information being referred to can be found elsewhere in the text, which shows that we can't understand language by looking at individual words or sentences. We have to analyse the text as a distinct linguistic unit in order to make sense of it. In the following section we will look in more detail at the five major categories of cohesion: reference, substitution, ellipsis, conjunction and lexical cohesion.

Reference – personal reference

Halliday and Hasan (1976) list three types of reference: personal, demonstrative and comparative. Personal references are those which, not surprisingly, are often used to refer to people.

Subjects – I, you, he, she, it, we, they
Objects – me, you, him, her, it, us, them
Possessive modifiers – my, your, his, her, its, our, their
Possessive heads – mine, yours, his, hers, its, ours, theirs

Of course these don't all have to refer to people. *They* could refer to *chairs*, *them* could refer to *snakes* and *it* could refer to almost anything except people, but it is easy to remember these by recalling that they often refer to people. (To be fair, we do sometimes call people *it*. When you answer the phone, you might ask, "Who is it?" and not mean to give offense. On the other hand, asking someone, "Do you know it?" while pointing at another person would be quite rude.)

It is important to mention that these words are sometimes called **pronouns**, as your school teacher might have called them. You may wonder if what you learnt in school was wrong, but the answer is "No." We can talk about things using different words, depending on what we want to explain. Sometimes it is correct to call me a father, sometimes a husband, sometimes a man and so on. Similarly, *I*, *you* and the other words are pronouns when we want to describe them in some situations, but when we want to call them by what they do, **personal reference** is the best term because they commonly *refer* to *people*.

Personal references have all of those properties that were explained earlier. (When I talked about *him* earlier, I was talking about personal reference, although I did not use the term.) They presuppose that their antecedents can be found outside the text (exophoric reference) or inside the text (endophoric reference). If the antecedent is inside the text, it will be found either earlier in the text (anaphoric reference) or later in the text (cataphoric reference). In all of these cases, the personal reference is interpretable as meaning something specific.

Generalised exophoric references are a special type of reference that are used to refer to everyone or to unspecified people. These commonly appear in aphorisms like "One never knows what might happen", where the reference *one* refers to people in general, not to any specific person in the text. *They* is also often used this way, such as in "They say it's going to rain." Who says so? Meteorologists on television? The newspaper's weather reporters? No specific person or people are referred to, but we are not really concerned with who specifically, so we just use *they* to point generally at someone who might likely have said it.

Extended text references are those where *it* is used to refer to a larger section of text than just a word or phrase. Compare the meaning of *it* in the following two examples, a modified version of an example found in Halliday and Hasan (1976).

1.3
1. He lost his phone. It was expensive.
2. He lost his phone. It was pretty careless.

In 1.3.1 *it* refers to "his phone", a noun phrase. This is personal reference. Note that it wouldn't matter if the first sentence of 1.3.1 was "He lost his expensive black Samsung phone." In this case *it* would refer to more words of the co-text, "his expensive black Samsung phone", but this is still just a noun phrase. In 1.3.2, however, *it* refers to more than just the phone. Here, *it* refers to the act of "losing his phone". This is extended text reference, as it refers to both the verb "lost" and the noun phrase "his phone" together.

Exercise – personal reference

Identify personal references in the following sentences. Decide whether the references are anaphoric (pointing back in the text), cataphoric (pointing forward in the text) or exophoric (pointing outside of the text). Identify what the references presuppose.

1. When a man is tired of London, he is tired of life. – Samuel Johnson
2. Just do it. – Nike
3. Before she went home, Sally had to say goodbye to Ellen Ferguson. – Kit Reed

Exercise – personal reference (commentary)

In sentence 1 the anaphoric personal reference *he* presupposes *a man*. More accurately we should say that *he* presupposes "a man who is tired of London", as *he* doesn't refer to men generally; only those who are "tired of London" must also be "tired of life." Anaphoric reference is much more common than cataphoric reference in most texts.

In sentence 2 *it* is an exophoric reference. It doesn't refer to anything in the text. Readers are free to decide for themselves what they should "Just do." Exophoric references are common in advertisements: "Because I'm worth it" (L'Oreal), "I'm lovin' it" (McDonald's) and "Have it your way" (Burger King). In all of these cases it is left for the reader to decide what *it* refers to.

In sentence 3 *she* is a cataphoric reference that presupposes *Sally*, or more specifically "the Sally that had to say goodbye to Ellen Ferguson". It's always good to remember that references are very specific. No other *Sally* is referred to here, only this specific one.

Reference – demonstrative reference

this, that, these, those, here, there, now, then, the

Demonstrative references usually refer to things in terms of their proximity to the text's producer. (For convenience, we can refer to a speaker or writer of a text as the **producer**, and the listener or reader as the **receiver**.) If I say, "Look at this", you know to look somewhere near me. If I say, "Look at that", you know to look somewhere other than near me. It's helpful to remember that demonstrative references often point at (or demonstrate) where something is. These references are **selective**, as they force the user to choose to identify something as being near or far. Using *this* is more precise than *that* because *this* means "near me", but *that* means "anywhere except near me."

It is important not to confuse the demonstrative *that* with the **relative pronoun** *that*. The relative pronoun *that* in a sentence like "The dog that we saw was really old" is not pointing at anything. In this sentence *that* joins "We saw a dog" and "The dog was old" into one sentence. Remember that the demonstrative *that* points while the relative *that* joins.

This and *that* can also be used as either heads or modifiers. **Heads** are the main or only words of phrases. In "Look at this" the word *this* is a head. **Modifiers** are words that accompany other words, giving more information about heads. In "Look at this pen" the word *this* is a modifier as it tells us more about which pen to look at. (*Pen* is a head in "Look at this pen.")

The word *the* is also a demonstrative as it is used to point at things. However, *the* is **non-selective**, as it doesn't tell us about how proximal (close) or distal (far) the referent is. Compare *this pen*, which points to a pen that is close to me, *that pen*, which points to a pen that is not close to me and *the pen*, which points to a specific pen, but without explaining whether or not it is close.

People learning English are sometimes confused by *the*, because some languages only have selective demonstrative references like *this* and *that*, so speakers of those languages are used to always selecting references based on distance. They're not sure about *the*, which doesn't let you choose how far away something is. On the other hand, English is not as precisely selective as some other languages, which have three selective demonstrative references. In Japanese and Korean, to name two examples, speakers must select between "near me", "near you" and "not near me or near you". When I learnt to speak some Japanese, I often said things like "Look at that (near you) speeding car" when I meant "Look at that (not near you) speeding car." I think I made a lot of Japanese people nervous.

This and *that* are not only used to point at physical items like pens and cars. These demonstratives can also be used to point at identifiable sections of text. If I say, "Listen to this", the demonstrative *this* refers cataphorically forward in time to whatever I'm about to say. After I finish talking, my wife might say, "I've already heard that", where *that* refers anaphorically back in time to whatever I just said. In the following sentence from Margaret Atwood's *Oryx and Crake*, think about how readers would interpret the word *that*: "She can hear him, he needs to believe that, but she's giving him the silent treatment." Readers know *that* presupposes "she can hear him", so Atwood doesn't have to write it again.

There are other demonstrative references. *Here* and *there* are usually used to point at physical locations. If I say, "Look over here", you must be able to see me to interpret where *here* is. This is an exophoric reference as the word *here* refers to the context in which I say it. If I send you an email saying "Let's meet there at noon", you will know I'm using *there* to point at a place, but you'll need more information to interpret what *there* refers to. If your previous email to me suggested meeting at a restaurant called

The Fat Duck for lunch, you'll know that *there* refers to "at *The Fat Duck*" and nowhere else.

Note – demonstrative there and existential there

Don't confuse demonstrative reference *there* with the existential *there*, which appears in sentences like "There's a funny smell in this room." In this sentence *there* is used as a subject; it is not pointing at anything. "There's a funny smell in this room" means something like "A funny smell in this room *exists*." Similar uses of existential *there* appear in sentences like "There are three reasons..." ("Three reasons exist...") and "There was a game starting at 4 pm." ("A game starting at 4 pm existed.")

You can often distinguish the existential *there* from demonstrative reference *there* in spoken texts by the way they are said. Look at the word *there*, which appears twice in the first part of Shel Silverstein's poem *Bear in There*.

There's a Polar Bear
In our Frigidaire–
He likes it 'cause it's cold in there.

The first *there* is existential. It has a grammatical role as a subject, but doesn't mean anything other than "A Polar Bear exists in our Frigidaire." We can signal this when we talk by saying something like "Thur's a Polar Bear..." The first *there*'s unimportance in meaning allows us to say it quickly and with little stress. The second *there* is a demonstrative reference that presupposes "In our Frigidaire". We don't say "...cold in thur" for the second *there*; instead we say it clearly.

Now and *then* are also demonstrative references, but they refer to times. It's difficult to use *now* to mean anything other than "at the present time", but *then* can mean whatever time is specified elsewhere in the co-text or context. When my daughter says, "Pick me up after school", and I say, "See you then", I mean "See you when I pick you up after school."

Reference – comparative reference

The final category is **comparative reference**, in which one section of the text is interpreted by comparing it to some other section of the co-text. In the sentence "This tree is taller than that tree", we don't know the exact height of "this tree", but we know that on a scale of "tallness" it is taller than "that tree". It is tempting to say that the trees are being compared in terms of *height*, but there are other ways of measuring height (i.e. *shorter*), so it is best to recognise that *taller* compares the trees on a scale of "tallness" only. Comparative reference is also commonly used to compare on a scale of quantifiable units, as in "This tree is taller than three metres."

Comparative references are made through the use of the comparative forms of adjectives. In the case of the adjective *big*, for example, the base form is big, the comparative is *bigger* and the superlative is *biggest*. When a text producer uses the base form, *big*, as in "Use a big bowl" in a recipe book, readers are asked to interpret *big* in relation to their general knowledge of the size of bowls, but they are not asked to compare *big* to anything in the text. (Consider that it would be difficult to interpret "Use a *big* flange" if you don't know anything about the usual size of a flange.)

The superlative form, as in "Use your biggest bowl", asks readers to interpret *biggest* in relation to the context in which they are receiving the text. For each reader this will be different depending on the size of the bowls they possess. As with the base form *big*, *biggest* demands an interpretation based on something outside of the text.

The comparative form of the adjective makes reference to the co-text for interpretation. In the following pair of sentences how do readers make sense of *bigger*? "Use a big bowl to prepare the icing. Use a bigger bowl to prepare the batter." Readers will know that bowls can only be *bigger* in relation to other bowls. In this case the second sentence doesn't provide any point of comparison, but the first sentence does, leading to the interpretation "Use a bigger bowl (*than the big bowl used to prepare the icing*) to prepare the batter."

Not all adjectives use *er* in the comparative form. Some comparative adjectives are irregular, such as *good-better* and *bad-worse*. (*Far* and *old* are sometimes confusing as each has two comparative forms, *farther* and *further* and *older* and *elder*.) Some polysyllabic adjectives use the form *more+base form*, as in *more beautiful* and *more intelligent.* The general rule is that adjectives of one syllable use the *er* form and adjectives of three or more syllables use the *more+base form.* There is some ambiguity as to whether we should use *er* or *more+base* with two syllable words. Is the comparative form of *lovely* either *lovelier* or *more lovely*? Notice that William Shakespeare used *more lovely* while Russian painter Wassily Kadinsky used *lovelier.*

Shakespeare – Shall I compare thee to a summer's day? Thou art more lovely and more temperate.

Kandinsky – An empty canvas is a living wonder ... far lovelier than certain pictures.

(Keen-eyed readers will also have spotted that Shakespeare used *more+base* for *temperate*, which could be pronounced as a three-syllable word. You see now why I called the previous rule a "general" one.)

Take care to distinguish between *more* in the *more+base* form, which compares a quality (Shakespeare's *more lovely* compares *thee* to *a summer's day* in terms of "loveliness") and *more* on its own, which compares amounts. In the following example *more* compares the amount of *40 pounds* to the amount of *money we need*: "It's going to cost 40 pounds. We need more money."

Note – clauses

A **clause** is a subject and a predicate. A **predicate** is a verb and anything else that says something about the subject. So a clause is a subject, a verb and anything remaining that is related to that subject. In the following sentences the subjects are in bold and the predicates are in italics.

1. **Arianna** *plays piano beautifully.*
2. **My wife's brother's daughter** *has studied piano for ten years.*
3. **Jessica** *sang the song* and **Arianna** *played the piano.*

It's more precise to refer to clauses than to sentences, as one sentence can contain more than one clause. In sentence 3 above, there are two clauses, but it is only one sentence. Think of *sentence* as being a description of the orthography, that is, a sentence is a group of words starting with a capital letter and ending with **terminal punctuation**: full stop, question mark or exclamation mark. Think of *clause* as being a description of the grammar, that is, subject, verb and anything else that relates to that subject.

Recognising and analysing clauses are important to thinking about communication. In the NWA song *Express Yourself*, rapper Dr Dre says, "It gets funky when you got a subject and a predicate." I'm not sure about the "funky" part, but it is clear that to "express yourself" you do need both the subject and the predicate. If you're only given a subject, such as *the doctor*, you don't know what the doctor did. If you're only given a predicate, such as *gathered the grapes*, you don't know who or what did it.

Substitution

Substitution, like reference, is a form of cohesive relation in that different words, phrases and clauses are linked, joining them into a text-level linguistic unit. Only a few words act as substitutes. *One, ones* and *same* are **nominal substitutes**, which means they are words that can take the place of nouns. The verb *do* in all its forms – do, does, did, done, has done, has been doing and so on – is the **verbal substitute**, taking the place of verbs or parts of verbs. The **clausal substitutes** *so* and *not* take the place of clauses and parts of clauses.

Look at the word *one* in the following sentence from Bram Stoker's *Dracula*. What does the word *one* presuppose here? "I trust that your journey from London has been a happy one, and that you will enjoy your stay in my beautiful land." You'll see that the nominal *one* substitutes for the noun *journey* in this example.

Substitution is similar to reference in that one word presupposes another word or words, but reference and substitution are not the same. Compare the meaning of *it* and *one* in the following two examples.

1.4
1. I have a red pen. Do you want it?
2. I need my red pen. Do you want the blue one?

In 1.4.1, you've seen that *it* refers to "the red pen that I have". The personal reference *it* in the second sentence presupposes the exact same thing that was already mentioned in the first sentence. In 1.4.2, you've recognised that *one* in the second sentence substitutes for *pen*, but we are now talking about a different pen than the pen mentioned in the first sentence. Substitution involves **repudiation**, which means that we are still referring to the same general class of things, but to a different specific item in that class. In 1.4.2 the nominal substitute *one* repudiates *red* with *blue*, so we are still talking about pens, but a blue pen, not a red one. The substitute *one* presupposes the head *pen*, but repudiates the modifier *red*.

The nominal substitute *one* is not the same as the cardinal number *one*. **Cardinal numbers** are used for counting: one dog, two cats, three sheep and so on. Look at the following example sentences and determine what *ones* substitutes for. "I need my red pens. You can have the blue ones." Here you can see that *ones* substitutes for *pens* and repudiates *red* again, but we don't know how many pens we are talking about. The nominal substitutes are not counting things, but are instead replacing their antecedents.

Look at the sentences in 1.5, more examples from *Dracula*, and determine what *do* in 1.5.1 and *so* in 1.5.2 presuppose.

1.5
1. If this book should ever reach Mina before I do, let it bring my goodbye.
2. Lord Godalming had slipped away for a few minutes, but now he returned. He held up a little silver whistle as he remarked, "That old place may be full of rats, and if so, I've got an antidote on call."

In 1.5.1 *do* substitutes for "reach Mina" and repudiates *the book* with *I*. (The sentence is still about the general case of "reaching Mina", but the specific thing that is doing the reaching is now *I*, not *the book*.) This *do* is a verbal substitute. It doesn't have any meaning on its own, unlike the **lexical verb** *do* in "Do your homework, please" which means "perform" or "attempt to complete". We can only interpret the verbal substitute *do* in 1.5.1 by looking at its co-text "If this book should ever reach Mina".

In 1.5.2 the clausal substitute *so* presupposes "that old place may be full of rats". This is a clause because it contains both a subject "that old place" and a verb "may be". However, we can see that the substitute *so* should be read as "... and if that old place *is* (not 'may be') full of rats, I've got..." This is the repudiation.

The clausal substitute *not* functions as *so*, except that it changes the polarity of the clause it substitutes for. **Polarity** refers to whether the verb is positive ("It *is* almost time to go") or negative ("It *isn't* time to go yet"). Polarity doesn't have anything to do with whether the meaning is positive or negative, so "Fraser lost his job" displays positive polarity, even though Fraser will be unhappy about being laid off.

In 1.6, look at how the clausal substitutes *so* and *not* allow the someone to affirm or deny something without repeating an entire clause.

1.6
1. Lily: Is she going to the party?
    Ngozi: I think so. (*so* = "she is going to the party")
2. Lily: Is she going to the party?
    Ngozi: I think not. (*not* = "she is not going to the party")

It is especially noticeable here that *so* and *not* substitute for something someone else said. Substitution, like all cohesive relations in texts, doesn't only take place within the words that the producer uses. We can also make links between things we say or write and things others have said or written.

Ellipsis

Like substitution, ellipsis involves the replacement of one thing with another. However, instead of using words as substitutes, in ellipsis we replace words with nothing. This may seem odd in theory, but in practice we do it constantly. When you read "Mia went home and ate dinner" you know Mia did two things: *went home* and *ate dinner*. You interpret Mia as the subject of the verbs *went* and *ate*, even though Mia was only mentioned once. There is **nominal ellipsis**, the omission of a noun which can be found elsewhere in the co-text. The sentence could have been written "Mia went home and Mia ate dinner", but it was not necessary to do so because the subject of the second verb, *ate*, couldn't be anyone else but *Mia*. (Using *Mia* twice may in fact be somewhat confusing. We are so accustomed to nominal ellipsis in sentences like this that seeing *Mia* as the subject of *ate* may lead us to wonder if this is a different person also named Mia.)

We sometimes have trouble spotting these omissions when we read or hear language, probably because we are so used to interpreting ellipsis without thinking about it. Slowing down our interpretation of language to identify ellipsis is not something we normally do, but we certainly use ellipsis in speaking and writing quite commonly.

In the short novel *The Metamorphosis*, Franz Kafka describes a man's reaction to having been turned into a large insect. Look at the following excerpt and identify places where Kafka omitted the subject *he* from the words.

1.7
"He felt a slight itch up on his belly; pushed himself slowly up on his back towards the headboard so that he could lift his head better; found where the itch was, and saw that it was covered with lots of little white spots..."

You will have seen that *he* appears in meaning, although not in the words, before three verbs: (he) *pushed*, (he) *found* and (he) *saw*. Kafka relied on his readers' successful interpretation of ellipsis, making additional uses of *he* unnecessary.

As with substitution, there are three types of ellipsis: nominal ellipsis, verbal ellipsis and clausal ellipsis. It is **verbal ellipsis** when all or part of the verb is omitted, but is understood from the surrounding text. Similarly, **clausal ellipsis** entails the omission of an entire clause, or at least both the subject and the verb of the clause.

1.8
1. He said that he'd eaten sushi before. He hadn't, but it seemed embarrassing to admit the truth.
2. Over three hours the CEO talked about the company, changes to procurement procedures and new health regulations.

In 1.8.1 *eaten sushi before* has been omitted after "He hadn't" in the second sentence. This is verbal ellipsis because part of the verb *had eaten* has been omitted, but the subject *he* remains in the text. The second sentence is interpreted as "He hadn't (*eaten sushi before*), but it seemed embarrassing to admit the truth."

In 1.8.2, *the CEO* and *talked about* have been omitted before both "changes to procurement procedures" and "new health regulations" in the second sentence. This is clausal ellipsis as both the subject *the CEO* and the verb *talked* have been omitted. This is interpreted as "Over three hours the CEO talked about the company, (*the CEO talked about*) changes to procurement procedures and (*the CEO talked about*) new health regulations. We can see that the words *the CEO talked about* are optional in the text's written form, but are present in the text's meaning whether or not they appear.

Exercise – ellipsis

Identify examples of ellipsis in the following sentences. Explain which words are missing from the text. Think about which elements of the text (nouns, verbs or clauses) could have been inserted, but were omitted because the same words already appeared.

1. You can't deny laughter; when it comes, it plops down in your favorite chair and stays as long as it wants. – *Hearts in Atlantis* by Stephen King.
2. It does not do to dwell on dreams and forget to live. – *Harry Potter and the Philosopher's Stone* by J. K. Rowling.

Exercise – ellipsis (commentary)

To recognise the ellipsis in sentence 1, ask yourself "What stays as long as it wants?" The answer is *laughter*, so this is nominal ellipsis. The word *laughter* or the personal reference *it* could have appeared before *stays* but was omitted here as readers know the word is there in the meaning, if not in the actual text.

Sentence 2 could have been written as "It does not do to dwell on dreams and *it does not do to* forget to live." This is clausal ellipsis, as the subject *it* and the verb *does not do* have both been omitted. It was not necessary to write *it does not do to* twice, as readers presuppose the existence of the second one by looking back in the text.

Conjunctions

Conjunctions are used to show specific types of connection in texts. Comedian Rodney Dangerfield said, "My wife and I were happy for twenty years. Then we met." The temporal conjunction *then* shows that there is a time relation between the first sentence and the second, that is, the first one happened before the second one. Dangerfield's joke relies on the conjunction, as most listeners would likely assume at first that he meant he and his wife were happy together for twenty years after they met.

Although it is common for receivers of texts to assume that sentences heard or read first also come first chronologically, this doesn't have to be so. Consider "He let himself in quietly. First, of course, he had to find his door keys, not the easiest thing to do noiselessly in his current state." In the preceding sentences the second clause in the sequence, "he had to find his door keys", comes chronologically before the first clause "He let himself in…", as indicated by the temporal conjunction *first*.

The four types of conjunction and their simplest forms are as follows:

1. Temporal *then* (time relation) "I went home *then* I ate dinner." As explained above, *then* shows that the two events are linked in chronological sequence. (Don't confuse the temporal conjunction *then* in this example with the demonstrative reference *then* in "It starts at 5 o'clock. I'll see you *then*." Here *then* presupposes "at 5 o'clock.")
2. Causal *so* (cause-and-effect relation) "I went home *so* I could eat dinner." Here *so* shows that the first clause "I went home…" caused the possibility ("could") of eating dinner.
3. Adversative *but* (unexpected relation) "I went home *but* there was nothing for dinner." By using *but* the author makes it explicit that going home led to the expectation of eating dinner, which in this case was not possible ("nothing for dinner").
4. Additive *and* – adding relation "I went home. And before I knew it, dinner was served." Additive *and* is sometimes confusing.

People are tempted to say that *and* means *then* here because they guess that "going home" happened before the "serving of dinner". However, this is information the reader is inserting into the text based on knowledge of eating dinner at home. The *and* in the clause simply tells the reader to take the clauses as being related, or add them, but doesn't specifically say what kind of relation the two clauses have.

We can sometimes interpret the relation between clauses without a conjunction by relying on other available information. If you read "It's cold. Wear a jacket", you know that being cold is unpleasant and that wearing a jacket keeps you warm. You take the two clauses and attempt to make them coherent based on your knowledge of the world. (Coherence, the relation between texts and their receivers, as opposed to cohesion, the relation between words in a text, will be discussed in detail in the next chapter.) There is enough relation between *cold* and *jacket* that we could describe them as weak collocations of each other, which helps us see the relation between the clauses despite the fact that the conjunction is left implicit. The text's writer could also choose to make the relation between clauses explicit. In "It's cold, so wear a jacket", the causal conjunction *so* provides the explicit link between *cold* and *wear a jacket*. "Because it is cold, wear a jacket" shows the same relation, this time through the use of the causal conjunction *because*. In these examples the causal conjunctions *so* and *because* provide an explicit link, one that is visible in the text and doesn't only exist in the reader's mind, and so they are cohesive.

Lexical cohesion

Words are not only related to each other in terms of how they refer to or substitute for one another. **Lexical cohesion** is the term Halliday and Hasan (1976) used to describe how the *meanings* of words create links in text. Think about the word *duck*. What does it mean? You know some possible meanings, but without more co-text you can't say precisely. In a discussion of farm animals you will interpret *duck* as a bird as you will hear the names of other farm animals in the text. As you read a restaurant menu, you will interpret *duck* as a cooked meal as you will see the names of other foods listed. The duck that swims in a pond and the duck we eat are not the same thing, but the word *duck* on its own is not enough for us to know which sense is meant if I ask you, "What does *duck* mean?" You can only determine which sense of *duck* I'm using once you have a co-text to work with, words like *farm, cow* and *pond* or *restaurant, menu* and *beef.* (Of course, in an active children's game that includes words like *jump* and *run*, you will probably interpret *duck* as "lower your head".)

Words like *farm, cow* and *duck* are **collocations**, meaning they are words that tend to appear close to each other in texts. After we mention *farm* we don't have to mention *duck*, but *duck* is more likely to appear in the co-text of *farm* than other words like *helicopter, pastry* or *ninja*. This is not to say that *farm* and *ninja* can't appear together in specific types of text, for example in stories about feudal-era Japan, but we are unlikely to guess that such words would appear together in general texts.

Remember *collocation* by noting it has the word *location* in it. Collocations are words that tend to appear in the same place. Researchers in **corpus linguistics**, which is the simultaneous ana-lysis of large numbers of texts, can use computer programmes to determine how likely some words are to be collocations of other words. They can even see how close certain words will often be to other words. You don't need to have a computer to make such determinations, however, as it is often enough to rely on intuition. A mention of *farm* will allow you to predict the appearance of farm-related words because you already know quite a bit about what can be found and done on a farm, even if you aren't a farmer. Of course, your intuition could be wrong. Not all farms have *tractors, horses* and *fields*. In a text about *server farms* you'd see different colloca-tions: *computer, network, processor* and so on.

Some words are very **strong collocations**, meaning they are highly likely to appear together in texts, or even side by side. The opposite of *fresh breath* is usually *bad breath*, but the opposite of *fresh bread* is *stale bread*. These words collocate so strongly that mixing them around either sounds odd (*good breath*) or changes the meaning of what is being said (*stale bread* is old, but *bad bread* doesn't taste good). When you're learning a foreign language, it can sometimes be difficult to recognise that some word combina-tions don't exist because they are not common collocations, even though they may make sense together. *Circumstances* collocates with *unusual* ("unusual circumstances") quite often, but less often with *weird*, even though *weird* and *unusual* are **synonyms** (words that have the same or very similar meanings) in many ways. Native English speakers who are not familiar with the concept of collocation are sometimes at a loss to explain these patterns in English, even though they use the patterns precisely. A quick way to have a rough look at possible collocational strength is to google the two words while putting them in quotation marks. *Unusual circumstances* is more than ten times as common together as *weird circumstances*.

Other strong collocations don't necessarily appear side by side, but are highly likely to appear together. *Sons* collocates quite strongly with *daughters*, to the extent that people sometimes say things like "I have two sons but no daughters" when asked if they have any children. Mentioning *daughters* is unnecessary here – people will assume there are none if they are not mentioned – but the strong collocation between *sons* and *daughters* seems to bring the word *daughters* into a text with *sons* in it. Sons and daughters can be described as being in the same **collocational field**. They don't necessarily appear right together, but the mention of one makes the mention of the other more likely.

Determining the difference between strong collocations and weak collocations is not a precise distinction unless you first determine which frequencies will count as strong or weak. Corpus linguistics, in which precise, computer-aided counts can be made, is a powerful tool for making such distinctions, but not everyone has access to **corpora** (bodies of linguistic) and the software for doing so. Nevertheless, it can be useful to call collocations *strong* or *weak* to distinguish between them in a general way. *Sons* and *daughters* collocate strongly with *parents*. *Sons* and *daughters* are weaker collocations of *aunt* and *uncle*. A discussion of familial relations is more likely to mention someone's parents than their parents' sisters and brothers. Weaker still is the link between *sons, daughters* and *teachers*. Of course, people who are teachers may have sons and daughters, but when discussing *teachers* we are more likely to mention *students*.

Numerous useful terms exist for discussing the relations between some collocations more precisely. **Meronyms** are words that mean part of a thing, but are used to represent the whole. If you read "His car needed to be repaired. The engine was broken", you recognise that the two sentences are cohesive because an *engine* is a part of a *car*. *Car* and *engine* are collocations, but *engine* is more precisely a meronym of *car*. You would also recognise a link between *repaired* and *broken*, as *repair* and *break* are **antonyms**, words that have opposite meanings.

We often see that texts are lexically cohesive through **reiteration**, the mention of the same things more than once in the text. Sometimes this is as simple as direct **repetition**, using the same word twice. Seeing *run* in different sentences in a text is a clue that those sentences are related. Repetition includes different forms of a word: *run*, *ran*, *runner* and *running* are related even though they are not identical. These differences are described through **morphology**, (*morph* = "change", *ology* = "study of"). The *a* in *ran* indicates that this is the past tense of the present tense *run*, the *er* suffix on *runner* indicates that this is a noun ("person who runs") and the *ing* suffix indicates that this is either a gerund (a verb used as a noun) as in "Running is good exercise" or part of a present continuous verb, as in "The dog is running around the park." Despite the morphological differences, we can see that *run*, *ran*, *runner* and *running* are repetitions of the same essential meaning. (See Chapter 3 for a note on morphology.)

Reiteration also includes **synonymy**, which was previously described as the relation between words with the same meaning. *Child* and *kid* might be called synonyms as they both mean "young person". This is the **denotation**, or primary literal meaning, of those two words. However, like most synonyms these are not identical in all ways. *Child* may make us think or feel positively about the innocence and naivety of the people being described. These are the **connotations**, the feelings and non-literal meanings of the word. *Kid* has different, sometimes negative, connotations: rambunctious, overactive and troublesome. The movie *Kids*, about sexually active, drug-using young teenagers, likely took its name from these connotations of *kid*. (*Brat*, meaning "troublesome child", includes the negative feelings in its denotation, which has led friends of mine to refuse to buy their daughters *Bratz* dolls.) Synonyms are also sometimes different in how formal or informal they are. *Child* is more formal than *kid*, so a science textbook or doctor would be more likely to use *child*. (Even more formally, a child could be a "sexually immature human".) Synonyms are also not always the same in all senses of the words. In one sense, *kid* means "child", but in another *kid* means "young goat".

Finally, reiteration includes **subordination** and **superordination**. Subordinates are types of something, so a *Honda Jazz* is a subordinate of *car*, and *car* is a subordinate of *vehicle*. In this hierarchy, *Honda Jazz* is thus also a subordinate of *vehicle*. To describe the relationship between these words starting at the top of the hierarchy, *vehicle* is a superordinate of *car*, and *car* is a superordinate of *Honda Jazz*. Be careful about the distinction between **meronymy** and ordination; *engine* is a meronym of *car* because an engine is part of a car, but an engine is not a type of car, so it is not a subordinate of car.

The discussion of lexical cohesion is a discussion of content words. **Content words** are, as their name implies, those words that have at least some meaning on their own, without referring elsewhere in the text. These are the words in the word categories that tell us what the text is about: nouns, adjectives and adverbs. These words are **open-class words**, meaning we can add new words to these categories as times change, introduce new words such as *camera* and *computer* as new technologies are developed and introduce new words such as *selfie* and *Facebook* as new social practices arise that take advantage of those new technologies. Open-class words can easily be moved into new categories, as the noun *friend* did when people started using it as a verb in "I friended her on Facebook." (Linguistic conservatives may not like these changes, but they must acknowledge that they have happened.) You can often communicate simple thoughts using only content words, for instance by pointing at your stomach and saying "Hungry."

Function words are those which help with the grammar of sentences. These words don't make much sense on their own: articles, prepositions, auxiliary and modal verbs and so on. These words are largely **closed-class words**, meaning we don't easily add new words in these categories. You can certainly think of new content words you have learnt recently, perhaps even as you have been reading this book, but I doubt you can recall having come across a new preposition (*in*, *on*, *under*, *behind*, *to*, *of* and so on) since you first learnt English. The references and substitutes discussed earlier in this chapter are function words (and non-words, in the case of ellipsis), so they rely on co-text for their meanings to be interpretable.

The meaning of cohesion

Thus far in this chapter you have read about texts, and in particular how the study of cohesion provides us with accurate terms to use when we describe the relations between different parts of a text. This is not to say that you did not previously understand texts when you read them, of course, but as a linguist, and more precisely as a discourse analyst, it is important that you're able to describe these relations accurately. You can't analyse discourse, as it was described in the Introduction, without being able to analyse the relations between the words that make up the text of the discourse. Halliday and Hasan (1976) argue that it is especially important to recognise **non-structural cohesion**, which are those links that connect words in *different* sentences, as opposed to **structural cohesion**, which are those links that connect words *within* the same sentence.

So, for example, in "He had won the victory over himself", the penultimate sentence of George Orwell's novel *1984*, we know that *He* is the subject, *had* is an auxiliary verb-marking tense, *won* is the main verb, *the victory* is the object and *over himself* is a prepositional phrase that explains more about *the victory*. We can see the link between *He*, the first word of the sentence, and *himself*, the final word, partly because we know about grammar, but also because *himself* is a personal reference. This is structural cohesion.

Now look at that sentence and the final sentence of *1984* together: "He had won the victory over himself. He loved Big Brother." There are no grammatical links to rely on to see us the relation between the two sentences. The grammar of the first sentence ended at *himself*. Now, the only link between the two sentences is the *He* in the second one. This is non-structural cohesion. Despite the fact that the two sentences are grammatically independent from the other, we see them as part of one semantic unit called a *text*, which is, assuming we read the whole way through, Orwell's novel.

Exercise – cohesion

Find examples of cohesion in the following text, a recipe for chicken stew from the *BBC Good Food* website. A commentary on some of the cohesive links follows.

01 Heat the sunflower oil in a large pan. Use a larger one if you plan to double the
02 recipe to preserve some soup for freezing. Fry the garlic for 5 minutes, making
03 sure to stir it repeatedly. Pour in the stock slowly to avoid splashing. Then stir
04 in the potatoes and spices.
05 Add the chicken and boil the mixture. Stir in the carrots and remaining vegetables.
06 Cover the pan and simmer for 45 minutes. Make sure to stir the stew every few
07 minutes. Once the chicken is tender the stew is ready. Serve with fresh pepper.
08 Cool and freeze any extra soup, but use it within a month of freezing.

Exercise – cohesion (commentary)

reference
It (line 03) anaphorically presupposes *the garlic* (line 02).

The in *the mixture* points at "the mixture you have made by following the instructions up until this point", that is, the whole first paragraph plus *add the chicken* in line 05.

Larger compares "the pan you use if you plan to double the recipe" with the *large pan* mentioned in the first sentence of line 01.

substitution
One in line 01 substitutes for the head *pan*. The text continues to discuss the general class *pans*, but a different subclass, so *larger* repudiates *large*.

ellipsis
In line 05 we interpret the instructions as "Stir in the carrots and (*stir in*) the remaining vegetables" although the verb *stir* has been omitted before *the remaining vegetables*.

conjunction
The temporal conjunction *then* appears in line 03, linking "Pour in the stock…" and "…stir in the potatoes…" in a time sequence. Readers would likely interpret this as a time sequence based on their general knowledge of instructional texts, which typically link items in sequence. However, the author has chosen to make the sequential order clear here. (Temporal conjunctions could have been used in other places, such as before *fry* in line 02.)

lexical cohesion
Many of the words are collocations. *Pan*, *fry* and *oil* are all related to cooking. *Stock*, *soup* and *boil* are all related to liquids. *Carrots* and *potatoes* are subordinates of vegetables.

Spoken language

For much of history, written texts were seen as the most important form of human language while spoken texts were dismissed as relatively unimportant. Partly this had to do with the ephemeral nature of speech. It was hard to analyse things people said without having access to technology that allowed words to be recorded and carefully analysed. This was, in part, related to *who* could write. When the ability to write was limited to certain members of society, especially those with more economic and social power, it was inevitable that their written words were seen as more prestigious than the spoken words of socially weaker illiterate people. This had to do, in part, with *what* was written, especially the important religious texts that were painstakingly copied out by hand.

This is no longer the case. Spoken texts can be recorded, transcribed and analysed. Literacy is more common throughout many societies. Spoken language is now recognised as having an important social function, allowing people to develop and maintain social relations. In addition, it is recognised that linguistic innovation comes through spoken language. New words typically appear in speech long before lexicographers decide that they are common enough to be included in dictionaries. If we want to know about language, we can't dismiss spoken texts as minor, unimportant relations of written texts. At the very least, we have to acknowledge that most of us talk a lot more than we write. A study of university students by Mehl *et al.* (2007, p. 82) found that "women and men both use on average about 16,000 words per day". It would be very difficult to produce even an approximation of that number of written words in a day without resorting to writing nonsense or using a lot of repetition.

So far in this chapter I have mostly discussed written texts, so it is important to point out that the features of cohesion apply to spoken texts as much as to written texts. The words that make up political speeches, conversations at a café, lectures and so forth will all be cohesive or we would not recognise them as texts. Some spoken texts are similar to written texts in that they are **planned**, that is, prepared ahead of time. An important speech will often be written, rewritten and edited before it is delivered orally to an audience. Politicians who regularly deliver speeches are known for making the same supposedly offhand comments and jokes at the same time on each occasion that they make a speech. Their careful planning includes preparing their words in such a manner that they don't look completely planned. Television and radio news broadcasts, university lectures and songs are also planned spoken texts.

Other spoken texts are **spontaneous** events for which the participants don't prepare ahead of time: chance meetings with friends on the street, informal discussions at work and so on. When you make arrangements to meet someone for lunch, you know you will talk, but you might not have any thoughts about what you will talk about or how you will say it. Most of us are so well versed in participating in spontaneous spoken interactions that we don't think about them at all. It's only when we are asked to give a speech or make a presentation, both planned speech events, that we start to panic.

The line between planned and spontaneous texts is not clearly defined. Instead of picturing a strict delineation, it is best to imagine a continuum with completely planned texts at one end and completely spontaneous texts at the other. If you arrange to meet someone to tell them some interesting news about yourself, you may have some ideas about what you want to say, but you probably don't take too much time planning how you will deliver your news. You might call this a mostly spontaneous spoken text. On the other hand, a good lecturer will plan her words to an extent, perhaps using a PowerPoint presentation to show her plan to the audience, but she'll allow some spontaneity, taking questions and making remarks appropriate to her audience. This would be a mostly planned spoken text.

Written texts can also be described as planned or spontaneous. You spend more time preparing a university essay, job application or email to a co-worker than you do a text message to a friend or a note on the refrigerator reminding a family member to buy milk. We can generally say that spoken texts tend to be more spontaneous than written texts, but there is overlap between the two.

Most of the language education we receive is about planned written texts, although it may not be described as such. Teachers show students how to write sentences and essays, university lecturers explain how to write formal academic papers and career counsellors teach people how to write CVs and cover letters. The nature of spontaneous spoken texts is mostly left unexplained. Parents may give some explicit instruction on how to talk, reminding their children to say "please" when they make requests, for example, but for the most part we learn how to talk spontaneously without direct explanations.

Conversation

If we want to explain how language works, we must be able to discuss all texts, not just those planned written ones that were historically considered most worthy of study. Informal spoken conversations, which are probably the most commonly occurring speech event for the majority of people, can't be ignored. Sacks, Schegloff and Jefferson (1974) wrote what has become a very influential article to explain how we talk spontaneously. Although the title of their paper, *A simplest systematics for the organization of turn-taking for conversation*, is not particularly simple, their purpose is: explain what a conversation is and what rules people follow when they participate in one. Understanding Sacks *et al.*'s (1974) explanation of *conversation*, much as with Halliday and Hasan's (1976) explanation of *cohesion*, is fundamental to understanding the ways in which people use language.

To begin, it is important to define precisely what is meant by *conversation*. Sacks *et al.* (1974, p. 700–701) define it as a spoken interaction between a few speakers in which people mostly talk one at a time. Additionally, neither the topic, the number of turns each person will have, nor the length of each turn is set in advance. In practice, there is no set limit on how many people can be involved in a conversation, but once you pass a small number, typically given as four or five, it becomes difficult for everyone to have a turn, and some management, at least informally, is needed to make sure everyone has the opportunity to speak. Even small, relatively informal business meetings typically have a chair to keep speakers organised. Conversations among friends may sometimes become similarly managed once too many people are involved. The more common occurrence is for the group of friends to divide into two or more smaller groups of a size better suited to conversation: one group in the kitchen, another by the television, and so on. We can see that Sacks *et al.*'s definition of conversation is quite specific. Some spoken texts are not conversations: a political speech is given by one person, a lecture's topic is set in advance, a meeting's length is often predetermined and so on. However, as conversations feature so prevalently in our daily lives, they are a special type of spoken text that is worthy of special attention in linguistic analyses.

Sacks *et al.* (1974) have provided us with precise terms to discuss the units of language that make up spontaneous conversations. Planned texts, especially written ones, are divided into sentences, each of which is made up of a subject, a verb and optional additional elements. Conversations may include sentences, but they often don't. Conversations, instead, are made up of clause-length, phrase-length and word-length **turn construction units** (TCUs). Unlike in a written text, in which it is expected that we write in sentences, participants in a conversation use shorter units of language. In 1.9 identify which TCUs are clauses, phrases and words.

1.9

```
01 A: you want the book?
02 B: the older edition?
03 A: yeah
04 B: sure
05 A: good enough?
06 B: thanks
```

Turn 01 is the only clause TCU here. It features a subject *you* and a verb *want*. It is not spoken as a question grammatically, that is, A doesn't say "Do you want the book?" but we can recognise that it is a question from the inclusion of the question mark signalling rising intonation. (The distinction to be made here is between an **interrogative clause**, one which shows that it is asking something through grammar (e.g. "*Would you like* some coffee?"), and a **question**, which can be made without grammar (e.g. Saying "Coffee?" while holding up a pot.)

Turns 02 and 05 are phrase TCUs. *B*'s turn 02 is a noun phrase as it has a head noun *edition* and two modifiers: *the* and *older*. There is no verb, so it is not a clause, but we can interpret the phrase by looking at turn 01 and guessing that *B* is asking "Is it the older edition?" or perhaps "Do you want the older edition?" Speaker *A* must have arrived at a satisfactory interpretation as the response "yeah" in turn 03 allowed the conversation to progress. *A*'s turn 05 is also a phrase, likely interpretable as "Is that good enough?" or "Is it good enough?" as *B* responded with "thanks" and did not ask for additional clarification.

Turns 03, 04 and 06 are word TCUs. None of them would be interpretable in isolation – if you came around a corner to hear someone say "Yeah", you would not know what he or she responded to – but within this conversation, a spoken text in which each part relies on the rest of the text for its interpretation, they are all enough despite their brevity.

Sacks *et al.* (1974) also discuss sentence TCUs, but linguists often prefer the term *clause* to *sentence*. The term **sentence** does provide some information about **orthographical features** (capital letters, hyphens, punctuation, etc.) of the relevant words, as sentences are usually said to start with a capital letter, contain at least one clause and end with a terminal punctuation (that is, a full stop, question mark or exclamation mark). However, *sentence* doesn't tell us much about grammar, as "He walked home and ate dinner while she stayed and studied at the library" is only one sentence, but four clauses. Calling that a *four-clause sentence* (or *four-clause complex*) provides more information than just *sentence*.

Turn completion

We can also use 1.9 to think about *how* we know when speakers have finished their turns: grammar, intonation and action. Turn 01, as discussed, is grammatically complete as a clause because it has a subject *you*, a verb *want* and an object *the book*. A competent English user would hear this and realise that it is a fully formed clause that doesn't need any more words to be complete.

In addition, turn 01 was spoken with rising intonation, which signals that it is to be taken as a completed question. Rising intonation, when used in yes/no questions, typically begins at the start of the final syllable in the question. Transcribers may indicate this with an arrow rising from left to right (↗) before the last syllable of the question. I could have written "you want the ↗book" to make it clearer to readers that this turn was said with rising intonation. This is more accurate than using a question mark as I did in 1.9 because, although we use a question mark for different types of questions in written language, we don't use the same intonation for all questions. Yes/no questions are commonly signalled with rising intonation while wh- questions (who, what, where, when, why and how) are not. (Try saying "What day is it?" and "Is it Tuesday?" and notice that while you may rise on the syllable *day* in *Tuesday*, you don't rise anywhere in "What day is it?").

Finally, we can see that turn 01 was complete as an action, meaning that a receiver would understand *why* it was said. In this turn, it is simple as it is a question, but other actions could be responses, offers, warnings, statements of information and so on.

When a turn is completed, the speaker has created what Sacks *et al.* (1974) call a **transition-relevance place** (TRP), a point at which it is obviously possible for another speaker to begin speaking. Note that this doesn't mean another speaker *must* speak, only that a space in the text has been opened where a transition to another speaker *might* occur.

Look again at turns 02, 03 and 04 of 1.9 while considering how turns which are completed by grammar, intonation and action mark TRPs. (Rising intonation has been indicated with arrows for clarity.)

1.9

```
01 A: you want the ↗book (TRP)
02 B: the older edi↗tion (TRP)
03 A: yeah (TRP)
04 B: sure (TRP, no one chooses to speak, conversation ends)
```

Turn 02 is grammatically a noun phrase. Rising intonation on the turn indicates that it is to be taken as a yes/no question. As an action, it doesn't answer the question in turn 01, so it will be interpreted as a request for clarification about the question in turn 01. Turn 03 doesn't feature any grammatical relations between words as it is just one word. However, listeners will realise that there is an elliptical clause here, so turn 02 will be interpreted as something like, "yeah [it is the older edition]." No intonation is indicated in turn 03, yet without it turn 03 is still easily interpretable as an action for it is a response to the question in turn 02. Turn 04, despite also featuring only elliptical grammar ("sure [I want the book]") and no intonation, is also easily interpretable as an action, in this case a response to turn 01. The question in turn 02 is answered in turn 03, so a listener will look back to find an earlier turn to make turn 04 relevant as an action.

To clarify something written in the previous paragraph, it should be said that *all* speech features intonation, whether it is rising, falling or level, but transcribers typically only indicate features of intonation that they want to discuss. For most purposes, it would be too laborious to show all intonation contours. If spoken transcriptions don't show intonation, you should assume that the words were spoken in the most obvious way. In fact, this holds true for many features of conversation: pauses, volume, speed and so on. Transcribers rarely show all of them, choosing instead to focus on those which they think are most relevant to their current purpose.

Conversations take place among multiple speakers, but as conversations are spontaneous, there is no set order of turns that each participant must follow. Speakers instead allocate turns in two ways: **other-selection**, in which the current speaker indicates who should speak next, and **self-selection**, in which someone chooses to speak, despite no indication in the text that he or she should speak next.

Other-selection is often done through the use of a **vocative**, which is a person's name, title or other means of addressing a specific person. The name *Johnny* in "Johnny, be good" is a vocative as it is being used to talk to Johnny. The name Johnny in "Do you know Johnny?" is not a vocative as it is being used to talk about Johnny, not to him. In 1.10 some examples of other-selection by vocative are presented with the vocatives marked in italics.

1.10
1.   What do you think, *Abby*?
2.   *Nurse*, please pick up line 02.
3.   Excuse me, *sir*. You dropped your wallet.

In English we typically use commas in written texts or pauses in spoken texts to separate vocatives from the co-text. This marks them as distinct from other uses of the same words when they are being used to denote someone. Consider the difference between "Let's ask the nurse", meaning "Let's ask *the person who is a nurse*" and

"Nurse, please pick up line 02", meaning *"You who are a nurse, please pick up line 02."*

Other-selection is also done commonly by using the personal reference *you*, as in "Will you come with me?" In larger groups of people it is common to use gaze or to point with a finger to make it clear which person *you* refers to exophorically.

Self-selection occurs when cues from grammar, intonation or action make it clear that the current speaker's turn is finished, but there is no indication in the text about who should speak next. (Note that at the end of a completed turn that has no indication of who should speak next the current speaker may choose to continue speaking.) When someone greets you with "Hello", you know that to be polite you should reply with a greeting, but you haven't been specifically chosen to reply. In 1.11, speaker *E* says "See ya later" to a group of friends. Speaker *F* then self-selects to respond, followed by simultaneous self-selection by speakers *K*, *J* and *A*. (The square bracket [indicates that turns 03, 04 and 05 all began at the same time.)

1.11 (Data collected by Kirsten Marsh)

```
01 E: I'm off. See ya later
02 F: Bye babes
03 K: [Laters
04 J: [See ya tomorrow
05 A: [Bye
```

Conversations are texts, but they differ from most other text genres as they are spontaneously produced by their participants. Being able to identify TRPs, by understanding the construction of turns, turn completion and speaker selection, allows us to see how speakers work together to build these texts.

Exercise – turns

Identify the TCUs and TRPs in the following transcription. Explain whether turn-taking happens via self-selection or other-selection. A commentary on some of the features follows.

Two restaurant serving staff, J & K, discuss some of their customers.

```
01 J: Have you been to table eighteen
02 K: Yeah I took them a jug of tap water
03 J: Anything ↗else
04 K: No
```

Exercise – turns (commentary)

In line 01 *J* produces a clause-length interrogative TCU. Although it is grammatically a yes/no question, *J* did not produce it with any rising intonation. This is likely because the grammar of the clause makes it apparent that it is a question, so rising intonation would be possible, but redundant. This turn features other-selection, as *you* refers to *K*, thus selecting her to speak next.

Line 02, although one turn, should be analysed as two separate TCUs: the word-length TCU "Yeah" and the clause-length TCU "I took them a jug of tap water." The first TCU is an action that responds to *J*'s question in turn 01. (Note that "Yeah" here features clausal ellipsis, as we interpret *K*'s "Yeah" as "Yeah [I have been to table eighteen].") There is thus a TRP after "Yeah", as this turn is possibly complete; a question has been answered. However, *K* self-selects to continue speaking, producing the clause-length TCU "I took them a jug of tap water." This is a declarative clause that elaborates on *J*'s question in line 01.

J's phrase-length TCU in line 03 again features ellipsis, and is likely to be interpreted as "[Did you take them] anything ↗else". The rising intonation and the elliptical information help us interpret this as a new action. Although *J* has not said *you* in turn 03, we should see this as other-selection, as the elliptical *you* indicates that *K* should speak next.

The word-length TCU "No" in line 04 shows us that *K* has interpreted "Anything ↗else" as an action requiring a response. There is now a TRP after "No" in which either speaker could choose to continue the conversation. If neither one speaks, the conversation ends.

Thinking about the Meaning

In this chapter we begin to examine *discourse*, which encompasses the words of the text plus the context in which the text is produced. We look at how people make sense of the multiple possible meanings of language in use and at a useful tool for describing meaning in language.

Think about the meaning of the word *have*. It is a very semantically flexible English verb, so we can easily use it to mean many things. In *have a car* it means "to possess", in *have an argument* it means "to participate in", and in *have an ear infection* it means "to be afflicted with". We can't really say that any one of these meanings of *have* is the real meaning; we can only make sense of the word when we see it used.

This is a useful distinction. **Meaning** refers to what a word might possibly signify in any text, while **sense** refers to what the word signifies in the text we are looking at. De Beaugrande and Dressler (1981, p. 84) put it like this: "If *meaning* is used to designate the potential of a language expression (or other sign) for representing and conveying knowledge (i.e., virtual meaning), then we can use *sense* to designate the knowledge that actually is conveyed by expressions occurring in a text."

So *have* has many meanings, but its sense will depend on how it is being used in a text. This distinction between meaning and sense doesn't only apply to words; it can also apply to phrases and clauses. When I hear a student say "I have a class", I make sense of the clause as something like "I must attend a class", but when I hear a teacher say "I have a class", I make sense of it as "I must teach a class".

Of course, there are other semantically flexible verbs similar to *have*, such as *get*, *make* and *go*. We can *get something* (understand it) or *get something* (receive it), for example. However, *have* seems particularly productive in terms of the number of ways we use it.

Note – tense and aspect

Don't forget that sometimes *have* doesn't really mean anything, but instead has a grammatical function, as in "I have visited Paris". This *have* helps indicate that the lexical verb is present tense and perfect aspect, but the sense comes from the lexical verb *visit*.

English verbs have **tense**, meaning they can be present or past. **Regular past tense verbs** follow the pattern of "add *ed* to make a past tense", so we have *walk-walked, close-closed* and so on. **Irregular past tense verbs** follow different patterns or no pattern at all, so we have *eat-ate, read-read* and *think-thought*.

Verbs also have **aspect**, which tells us something about how verbs are related to the passing of time. A full analysis of tense and aspect is beyond the scope of this book, but a precise introduction to these terms would be useful. The distinction between tense and aspect is shown below using the verb *see* as an example.

	Simple aspect	Continuous aspect	Perfect aspect	Perfect continuous aspect
Present tense	see	seeing	have seen	have been seeing
Past tense	saw	was seeing	had seen	had been seeing

Continuous aspect is also sometimes called *progressive aspect*.

In the film *The Silence of the Lambs*, the fictional serial killer Hannibal Lecter relies on the semantic flexibility of *have* when he says, "I'm having an old friend for dinner." If we did not know anything about Lecter, we would likely make sense of this as "I am hosting an old friend for dinner." This is the most immediately interpretable sense of *have*. We make sense of it based on what we assume people usually mean by *have*.

Watchers of the film know that Lecter is not normal. He is a cannibal, so watchers interpret this as "I am eating an old friend for dinner." Using "having an old friend" helps portray Lecter as being devious with his words, it shocks viewers as they make sense of his words, and it also makes them feel clever as they realise they have discovered the proper sense. It's no surprise that this is one of the best-remembered final lines of a film.

Text and discourse

This example provides us with a useful place to look again at the distinction between *text* and *discourse*. The words "I am having an old friend for dinner" exist as part of the text, which in this case is the script of the film. However, we can also see the words as part of the discourse, which includes the script, the characters, the setting and everything else that helps us make sense of those words. We can even extend the meaning of discourse to include the audience's knowledge of the world outside the film. The film's creators know that the audience will have an understanding of normal human behaviour, an understanding that includes knowledge of cannibalism as an immoral and illegal taboo. As the words "I'm having an old friend for dinner" are received by an audience who know, by the end of the film, that Lecter is a cannibal, the words in the text acquire new significance as part of the discourse.

Some authors use the terms *text* and *discourse* almost interchangeably. Stubbs (1983, p. 9), for example, writes, "I do not propose to draw any important distinction between the two terms." Others, such as Jackson and Stockwell (2011, p. 1.3.4), argue that "it is perhaps more sensible, since both terms exist, to restrict discourse to spoken language and text to written language." I don't like either of these practices, but it is important that readers know the possible distinctions authors make so they can judge them for themselves and so that they are not confused when they read different explanations for what the terms mean.

I prefer Georgakopoulou and Goutsos's (1997, p. 4) explanation that "discourse is thus a more embracing term that calls attention to the situated uses of text: it comprises both text and context." Discourse is text in a certain context and each text can only be understood as part of whatever context it occurs in.

Look at 2.1, a short spoken interaction between two people. Can you make sense of this interaction as a text, without knowing more about the context? (Note that the same speaker produces both utterances.)

2.1

```
01 A: sorry, where's the entrance? I guess I shouldn't go past them
02 B: thank you
```

You can probably make some guesses at what happened here, but without knowing more about the context, that is, without knowing how this text existed as part of a discourse, you can't properly make sense of it. *A*'s first word-length TCU "sorry" (line 01) initiates the interaction by apologising for interrupting someone, *B*, who is standing outside the entrance to a university library where there is evidence of construction work being done.

The first clause-length TCU "where's the entrance?" (line 02) gives a reason for the interruption by making a request for information. We can surmise that *A* asked *B* because *B* was standing close to the library's entrance, thus making him a likely source of accurate information. *B* was also wearing a high-visibility safety vest of the type often worn by builders, marking him as a possible participant in the construction and so again marking him as someone with possible information. This extra contextual information, *B*'s clothes and his location, helps explain why *A* chose *B*.

The next clause-length TCU "I guess I shouldn't go past them" (line 03) provides a reason for *A*'s question. When standing outside a clearly marked entrance to a building, it might seem strange to ask where the entrance is, so *A* points out that he shouldn't "go past them", where *them* is interpretable to *A* and *B* as warning signs, saying "No entrance." Liddicoat (2007) uses the term **accountable** to describe situations like this. When we exhibit odd linguistic behaviour, such as asking for an entrance while standing outside an entrance, we often need to explain our odd behaviour. "I guess I shouldn't go past them" provides an account, or reason, for the accountable question "where's the entrance?" in this bit of discourse.

B's response to the apology, question and account is not visible in the text, but of course it was visible in the context. *B* pointed first at a headphone in his ear, then pointed down the road. Pointing at the headphone suggests *B* was explaining the reason for not speaking. Speaker *A* likely interpreted the pointing as something like "Sorry I can't answer you but I'm listening to someone on this headphone." (I also interpreted it this way, as I too was looking for the entrance.) The next gesture, pointing down the road, directed *A*'s attention to a sign that read "Entrance in back" and featured a large arrow pointing around a corner. Speaker *A* made sense of the gestures in this way, as he said "thank you" and walked towards the sign.

You may wonder why I have written some 400 words over several paragraphs to explain an interaction that took less than 10 seconds overall. This is what discourse analysts do. Real "language in use" interactions, whether spoken or written, are *fast*. We make judgements about what to say, what to write, what we are hearing and what we are reading very quickly, but the number of judgements we make within that time is high. It took me hundreds of words to explain a short interaction and I did not even explain everything. (Was *B* smiling, for example? If so, would we make sense of his participation in the interaction differently than if he was not smiling or if he was frowning?) Discourse analysis involves examining language by "slowing it down" to try to explain precisely what is happening. This type of analysis demands that we look at the words of the text, of course, but we must also account for the context.

Exercise – context

An awareness of context is also necessary for an interpretation of written texts. In the somewhat well-known example sentence "They fed her dog meat", you probably assume from your general contextual knowledge of the world that this should make sense as "They fed meat to her dog." However, it is possible that it would make sense as "They fed dog meat to her" in other contexts.

On the inside of my office door there is a small, circular blue sign that displays the following text:

Fire door
keep clear

Explain how context (the sign is on the inside of an office door) helps us to make sense of this sign.

Exercise – context (commentary)

Readers will interpret this sign partly based on where it is situated. Because the sign says "Fire door" and it is affixed to a door, readers will interpret this as "This is a fire door." This may seem self-evident, but imagine if the sign was accidentally dropped on a street. The noun phrase "Fire door" would no longer make sense in that context. You'd probably then ignore the sign, or look around to see which door it had fallen from, knowing that the context was not appropriate for the text.

The missing "This is…" is taken for granted in many texts, especially signs: (This is a) bus stop, (This is the) British Museum, (This is a) hand dryer and so on. Putting the sign in the proper context, one where the words of the text match the real-world referent to which the signs refers, eliminates the need for "This is…". The location of the sign takes the place of pointing in a spoken text, such as when one says "Richard" while pointing at a man to introduce him.

"Fire door" would then be taken as a reason for the instruction to "keep clear". "Keep clear" is an imperative clause, prompting readers to do something. Imperatives such as this can be seen as rude (no one likes to be told what to do), so a reason for the prompt, in this case the door's special status as a fire door, is given. This reason helps **mitigate**, or lessen, the severity of the prompt. Note that in a different context, such as in an emergency, an imperative is perfectly acceptable without mitigation. No one would think you rude if you shouted "Run!" when there was a fire, for example.

Readers will be aware of the dangers of fire in most contexts, so they will accept the prompt to "Keep clear" for the reason given, but only when the sign is in the proper place.

Coherence

In the previous chapter we discussed cohesion, the links between words and how these links contribute to our understanding of language. In this chapter we begin by examining the concept of **coherence**, which is the term for those links that exist between the text and the text's receivers' ability to make sense of the words. The word *have* on its own is not coherent. We can't make sense of it. Only when it appears with more co-text, as in *have lunch*, can we make sense of it, thus making an invitation like "Let's have lunch next week" coherent. Similarly, a builder pointing down a street is not coherent on its own. We can only understand that he means "The entrance is that way" if we have heard the co-text and have seen the context.

Sometimes people speak incoherently: when dazed from a head injury, when mumbling while sleeping or when slurring while drunk. We hear their words and recognise them as being potentially meaningful, but we can't make sense of them. These may seem like obvious examples, but all language is potentially incoherent. I once had a confusing conversation with a co-worker. We'd greeted each other a few times in passing, but had never stopped to talk and introduce ourselves. Our first chat included the following segment. (**Segment** means "part of a conversation", that is, more than one turn, but not the whole conversation.)

2.2
```
01 S: I'm Sean what's your name?
02 E: Ahmed
03 S: hello Ahmed
04 E: no, Ahmed
05 S: sorry Ahmed
06 E: no I'm Ed
07 S: oh oh I'm Ed pleased to meet you Ed.
```

Here in turn 03 I made sense of his name as *Ahmed* with the stress on the first syllable, which I think is the most common English realisation of the name. (**Realisation** here means "to make real". We can realise the letters "minute", for example, as two different words. One of them means "60 seconds" and one of them means "tiny".)

In turn 04 I made sense of his name as *Ahmed* with the stress on the second syllable, partly because he started turn 04 with "no" and partly because he realised what I thought of as *Ahmed* with a different stress pattern. (The underlined syllable in *Ahmed* is pronounced more forcefully, but not necessarily louder.) I was still wrong. Only in turn 07 was I able to accurately make sense of what he had said, signalling that I had done so by repeating "I'm Ed" as part of my turn.

You may think that I'm not a very good linguist if I can't handle even a simple exchange of names properly. In my defence, I think there were three things that made me make sense of his turns incorrectly. Looking only at line 02, for example, I first made sense of his turn as an elliptical clause meaning "(My name is) Ahmed." Second, this interpretation of the ellipsis made sense as a complete turn in terms of action, that is, he answered my question from line 01. Third, his accent made his realisation of "I'm Ed" similar to *Ahmed*. We could use the international phonetic alphabet (IPA) to show precisely how he pronounced his words, but unless you already know the different symbols of the IPA, this would not be so useful. However, even without using the IPA, I don't think you should find it difficult to pronounce both *Ahmed* and *I'm Ed* in a way that makes them sound similar.

What Ed and I were doing in 2.2 was negotiating to make the discourse coherent. Normally we don't see the negotiation being done like this. When we successfully make sense of language we just keep talking or keep reading; there's no need to stop and discuss or think about which sense might have been meant. It's only when we need more help to make sense that such negotiation becomes part of the process of creating coherence.

There is a whole category of misheard song lyrics called *mondegreens*, which include examples such as "all of the other reindeer" from *Rudolph the Red-Nosed Reindeer* being misheard as "Olive, the other reindeer" and "Excuse me, while I kiss the sky" from Jimi Hendrix's song *Purple Haze* being misheard as "Excuse me, while I kiss this guy." In these cases, and others like them, listeners can't interrupt the singer to negotiate meaning as I was able to do with Ed. Listeners have to make sense on their own, thus leading to nonsensical alternate lyrics.

The ideational metafunction

Halliday (2004) provides us with a useful tool for distinguishing between possible meanings of words, and thus for explaining how we make language coherent. He explains that when we speak and write we use words to represent ideas and experiences. There is more than one way to describe any idea or experience, so we have to make choices about what we say or write. Imagine, for example, that you see two people wearing suits shaking hands in an office. How could you describe this event? You have to make choices about the language you use to describe that seemingly simple experience.

two people shook hands
a man and a woman shook hands
a black man and an Asian woman shook hands
two people in suits made a deal
a business meeting ended

All of these are possible, as would be many more choices. Do you describe the event as a very short event (a handshake) or as part of a larger event (business meeting)? Do you describe the people very generally (a man) or in detail (a tall, balding, black man in a blue suit)? Do you describe where they are, how they are posed, the expressions on their faces, or not? The list of things you could say is potentially very long, so you make choices. If you did not, you could end up talking all day as you described the minutiae of your experience.

Once you have made your language choices about the idea or experience you wish to describe, we can analyse the language you used in terms of how it represents those ideas and experiences. This is the essence of Halliday's ideational metafunction, a short list of six possible choices that you make for each clause that you produce. You can mostly ignore the prefix *meta* in the word *metafunction*. Just remember that language has a *function* of representing *ideas*.

Before giving the list of six choices (Halliday calls them *processes*) in full, let's look at an example that shows how this tool is useful in distinguishing between possible meanings and actual senses of words. Explain the sense of *call* in the two sentences in 2.3.

2.3
1. Call me Ishmael.
2. Call me tomorrow.

In 2.3.1, the opening line of Herman Melville's novel *Moby Dick*, the narrator invites us to call him by his name, which is Ishmael. Here *call* has the sense of "say my name as". (People use this sense of *call* when they say things like "My name is William, but you can call me Bill.") In 2.3.2, you realise that the person's name is not "tomorrow" and that instead the sense is "use your telephone to contact me tomorrow." This is obvious, but it's interesting to think about how you know this. You know that the word *tomorrow* is not usually a name, but you also could probably hear the difference in the way the speaker realises the final word.

Notice that you could make two identical groups of words mean different things by realising them differently. "Call me Ishmael" ("Call me by the name of Ishmael") could be distinguished from "Call me, Ishmael" ("You, Ishmael, should use your telephone to contact me") by varying the intonation and by pausing, as represented by a comma.

The two sentences in 2.3 are similar in several ways: both are made up of three words, both begin with the imperative form of the verb *call*, both have the object *me* following the verb and both have one additional word following *me*. The difference between the two final words, *Ishmael* and *tomorrow*, cause us to make sense of *call* in different ways.

Halliday's ideational metafunction provides us with a useful tool for clarifying the difference between these two senses. He explains that we should think of each verb in a clause as representing one of six possible processes. *Call* in "Call me Ishmael" is a verbal process, meaning it is a process that involves producing sound with your mouth: saying, speaking, singing, shouting and so on. Call in "Call me tomorrow" is a material process, meaning it is a process that involves physical action: jumping, kicking, swimming, driving and so on.

The six processes

01. Material processes – Verbs of doing, such as *jump*, *kick* and *drive*. These are verbs in the sense that most people describe them; someone is doing something physical.

02. Mental processes – Verbs of thinking and feeling, such as *wonder*, *love* and *worry*. These are verbs in which something is being done, but the process can't be seen by outsiders.

03. Verbal processes – Verbs of saying, such as *talk*, *sing* and *shout*. "Verbal" here is in the sense of "relating to words", not in the sense of "nouns and verbs".

04. Relational processes – Verbs of being, such as *be*, *seem* and *appear*. Verbs of this type often don't mean anything; they just show a relation between two things. The verb "is" in the film title *Life Is Beautiful* is not describing a process involving action of any sort; it simply relates a concept, *life*, with an attribute, *beautiful*. When we learn another language we can often skip over relational processes and still make ourselves understood. I can say, "I… Sean" and "I… hungry" and you can guess that I'm omitting *am*. This doesn't occur if I try to skip over other processes. If I were to say, "I… Buckingham Palace" it is impossible to know if the missing verb is *saw*, *visited*, *photographed* or something else entirely.

05. Behavioural processes – Verbs of conscious but often invisible action, such as *stare*, *listen* and *watch*. Think about the difference between *hear* and *listen*. They both relate in meaning to our aural sense, but *hear* is used for unconscious, unfocused processes, while *listen* implies that the process is conscious, focused and intentional. We might ask "Did you hear that?" after a strange noise is produced from somewhere. We're asking if the noise was heard, despite the fact that it was unexpected. *Hear* is usually a mental process. This is different from when we use "Listen to this", which prompts someone to consciously focus their aural sense. *Listen* is a behavioural process. Halliday called behavioural processes "minor processes". I like to think of these processes as minor in that they are less common, but also less clearly defined than other processes.

06. Existential processes – Like behavioural processes, Halliday called these processes "minor" ones. The word *existential* frightened me when I first encountered it as I associated it with the existentialist philosophy of Sartre and other philosophers, but it simply means "related to existence". These are verbs that point out the existence of something. As discussed briefly in Chapter 1, "There's a funny smell in this room" means something like "A funny smell in this room *exists*." The word *there* is the subject of that sentence, but it doesn't mean anything. *There* and *is* work together to mean *exists*. Existential processes will typically begin with *there* and be followed

by a form of the verb *be*. The Smith's song title *There Is a Light That Never Goes Out* means "A light that never goes out exists."

Exercise – processes

Identify the process in the following sentences. Consider how being able to group the processes into one of six categories makes explaining these bits of discourse easier.

1. Raskolnikov felt sick. – *Love love love* by The Mountain Goats
2. He felt the table's grain.
3. Darling, you look wonderful tonight. – *Wonderful Tonight* by Eric Clapton
4. Winnie the Pooh looked round to see that nobody was listening. – *Winnie-the-Pooh* by AA Milne

Exercise – processes (commentary)

In sentence 1, *felt* is a mental process. (Remember that despite the name *mental*, these processes include emotional and physical states.) The word *felt* here could be replaced with *was*, a form of the most common relational process *be*, without changing the sense of the sentence too much: "Raskolnikov was sick."

In sentence 2, *felt* is a material process. This *felt* means "the act of touching". Note that if you replaced *felt* with *was* here ("He was the table's grain") the sense would change completely, so this is not a relational process.

Look in sentence 3 is a relational process. No looking in the sense of "examining with eyes" is involved in the process. Of course you may suppose that the speaker had to look with his eyes before he said this, but the relational process *look* doesn't mean that. Instead, it means something akin to "Darling, *your appearance is* wonderful tonight", which shows us the basic relational process *is*.

In sentence 4, *looked* (or more precisely *looked round*, as this is a **phrasal verb**) is a behavioural process. Winnie-the-Pooh is actively "examining with his eyes", but there is not enough action for this to be classified as a material process.

As we have discussed, Halliday used the term *process* to allow distinction between different types of verbs. He made further distinctions between the *participants* in sentences, that is, the people or things that are doing those processes or that are having the processes done to them. In short, there is a difference between the *I* in "I am Sean", which is not doing anything except "being Sean" (Halliday called this *I* a *carrier*), and the *I* in "I am running", which is an *I* that is doing an action (Halliday called this *I* an *actor*). In this case, *I* represents a different idea in each sentence, despite the fact that both *I*s are functionally identical in that they are both first-person subject pronouns.

Sometimes, despite being different in function, a participant represents the same idea. *The apples* in "I ate the apples" and "The apples were eaten by me" are the same in that both are the *goal* (Halliday's word) of the material process *eat*. The apples in both of these sentences represents the same idea; they are the thing that was eaten. However, in "I ate the apples", *the apples* is the object of the sentence, while in "The apples were eaten", *the apples* is the subject of the sentence. These sentences are grammatically different, hence *the apples* change from object to subject, but they don't change the ideational meaning of *the apples*.

There are more than twenty names of participants in Halliday's list (see Halliday (2004, p. 260) for the full list), so learning them is useful if you want to very precisely describe how language presents ideas. For the purpose of discourse analysis, knowing the names of the six different processes is sufficient for describing different types of discourses. Different types of languages in use may feature a noticeable number of processes of one type. A newspaper article about a new government policy may feature a number of verbal processes: "The government *announced*...", "The opposition *claimed*...", "Analysts *suggested*..." and so on. A lecture may feature numerous relational and existential clauses: "This *is* the source...", "She *was* the first to...", "*There are* four known cases..." and so on. Simple narratives often are based on material processes: "Jack and Jill *went*...", "Jack *fell* down and *broke*...", "Jill *came*..." and so on.

This is not to suggest that speakers and writers are limited to certain types of processes depending on the nature of the discourse they produce. Only the simplest of texts, such as the nursery rhyme *Jack and Jill* (which you will have recognised in the previous paragraph), will be so specifically organised in terms of the ideational metafunction. However, using the ideational metafunction does give analysts a precise tool to use when they want to explain what a text is about, meaning what types of ideas and experiences are being expressed in the discourse. This tool, combined with the cohesive relations described in Chapter 1, allows us to say clearly what kind of discourse we are analysing. Instead of relying on general feelings about the topic, we can use accurate **metalanguage** (language used to talk about language) to explain the discourse.

An encyclopaedic entry about penguins, for example, will likely feature repetition (*penguin – penguins*), superordination and subordination (*birds – penguins*), meronymy (*penguins – wings*) and collocations (*penguin – Antarctic – ocean – swim*). The processes related to the penguins' characteristics and their behaviour will likely be relational ("Penguins *are*...", "These birds *seem*...") and material ("*swim*", "*can't fly*"). Other types of processes may be related to scientific analyses of penguins ("*were researched*", "*have been observed*"). Non-specialists would certainly recognise the topic of an encyclopaedic entry about penguins; linguists will use the appropriate metalanguage to isolate salient features that help make the topic coherent.

Exercise – words, clauses and ideas

Choose a news article, a restaurant or film review, or other short text of a few hundred words. Identify words and processes that show the topic of the text. Describe the relationship between words in terms of cohesion. Do the grammatical and lexical links clearly indicate the topic? Next, describe the meaning of clauses in terms of the ideational metafunction. Think about which types of processes are associated with which parts of the text. For example, a film review might feature material processes when discussing the plot of the film, but mental and relational processes when the author discusses his or her opinion about the film.

Schema

Horton, a friendly elephant in Dr Seuss' *Horton Hatches the Egg*, is well-known for repeating "I meant what I said and I said what I meant." This simple explanation of communication, that we mean things and are consequently able to say or write them, is probably not true. Horton may know what he wants to say, but it would often be impossible for him to say everything that he wants to. We almost inevitably must say *less* than we mean.

To begin thinking about this, it may be useful to look at the following three sentences and think about the different images they produce in your mind. (Sentences and explanations modified from Anderson *et al.* (1977, p. 368).)

2.4
1.   The baby kicked the ball.
2.   The goalkeeper kicked the ball.
3.   The golfer kicked the ball.

Each of these sentences is grammatically similar. A noun phrase (*The baby, The goalkeeper, The golfer*) acts as a subject of the past tense simple aspect verb *kicked*, followed by the direct object *the ball*. However, the "kicking a ball" event that a receiver of these sentences will imagine will be quite different in each case. First of all, the balls themselves are imagined differently: a toy ball for the baby, a football for the goalkeeper and a golf ball for the golfer. If the sentence's author wanted readers to imagine a different kind of ball, it would have to be made explicit. For example, "The goalkeeper kicked the tennis ball" could overwrite the default expectation of "football".

I realise that, depending on your personal sport preferences, you may associate *goalkeeper* with ice hockey, lacrosse, water polo or some other sport. That's fine, of course, as the point of this discussion is that we each interpret language based on our own knowledge of the world. I can't force you to accept *goalkeeper* as being a football player when there are other types of goalkeepers. I can, however, make a judgement about a general audience and assume that, since football is usually said to be the world's most popular sport, most readers will associate goalkeepers with football.

Returning to the three sentences, the verb *kicked* will also have been pictured differently when picturing each of them. What kinds of kicks were these? The baby's kick was probably accidental, as babies don't have much fine motor control and may flail about a bit. The goalkeeper's kick was probably strong and had a purpose within the confines of the game. The golfer's kick, while possibly also strong, was not within the rules of the game. (Even non-golfers usually know that players must hit the ball with the club.)

Anderson *et al.*'s (1977) three sentences are somewhat well-known within computer programming and artificial intelligence circles. Human readers of those sentences can easily picture different senses for "kick" and "ball", while computers struggle to do so. We are not relying only on the words we see in the text, *kicked* and *ball*, but also on our knowledge of the various contexts in which balls are kicked. As Anderson *et al.* (1977, p. 369) put it, "Every act of comprehension involves one's knowledge of the world as well."

So people, and Horton the elephant, can't simply say what they mean. We have to rely on our listeners and readers already knowing things. We make judgements about who we are talking to or writing for, think about what kind of knowledge they already have, then proceed while keeping that knowledge in mind. In other words, we rely on **schema**, the mental picture or plan that people have about a topic or process. This is related to the term *schematic*, a technical drawing, or *scheme*, a plan for getting something done, but *schemata* are those mental plans we hold in our heads about how the world and parts of it function. (Note that the plural of *schema* is sometimes given as *schemas*, but I prefer using *schemata* as I think it makes me sound clever.) The term *schema*, often associated with Bartlett (1932), is nicely explained by Schank and Abelson (1977, p. 41), who make the point that you can "leave out the boring details when you are talking or writing, and fill them in when you are listening or reading" (p. 41).

If I tell you that "I take the subway to work, but today I forgot my travel pass", I'm leaving out numerous "boring details": people often don't work at home, people travel to work, subways are a form of transportation, people usually must pay for public transportation, one way to pay is to purchase a pass that is good for a set period, and so on. If I did tell you all of this you'd think I was being ridiculous, treating you like a child who did not know anything. But of course you're not a child, so I can rely on your schematic knowledge of work and transportation and subways to communicate much more than I actually said. I can use your knowledge to take a shortcut and present you with an abbreviated version of what I mean, then rely on you to make sense of it. You will then make sense of the purpose of my utterance, by guessing that I did not take the subway to work today, because I wasn't able to pay for it.

Communicating by relying on schematic knowledge is more than just knowing the words. In my previous example you did not just need to know what a *subway* or *travel pass* is, you need to know how those two things work, how they relate to each other and how they relate to what I'm trying to tell you, which was that I did not take the subway today, despite usually doing so. You may not know the word *subway* in Korean {지하철 *jihacheol*} or German {*U-Bahn*}. Similarly, you might not know that English-speakers in London call the subway the *Tube* or that in Washington it is known as the *Metro*, but you would have a good general knowledge of how they work once you have heard their names.

Schemata are said to be hierarchical. Your understanding of "I take the subway to work, but today I forgot my travel pass" is based on your understanding of the subway, which is based on your understanding of public transportation, which is based on your understanding of transportation and so on. When you think about how you want to communicate with someone, you must make assumptions about how far up or down that hierarchy you think your recipient's schematic knowledge will extend. Teachers often have the problem of understanding what schema knowledge their students have. An astronomy teacher who wants to teach about the movement of the planets will know about physics, gravity and so on. But before teaching these things to students, he or she will have to consider what schematic knowledge the students have. Do they understand gravity? Do they know what planets are? Do they understand that the Earth is a planet? A teacher who assumes too little schematic knowledge will bore the students by repeating things they already know, but a teacher who assumes too much schematic knowledge will confuse the students by skipping over things they need to know.

We can therefore make judgements about the nature of the discourse by thinking about how the information presented explicitly in the words of the discourse compares to the information that is implicitly assumed to be there. Is the information presented quite explicit? If so, the producer of the discourse may not be assuming much about the schematic knowledge of the audience.

Compare the following two bits of discourse in 2.5. (Example 1 is modified from Schank and Abelson (1997).)

2.5

1. John went into a restaurant. He ordered a hamburger and a Coke. He asked the waitress for the check and left.
2. Kazuhisa went into a restaurant. He got his ticket from the machine. After he ate his *gyudon* he went back to work.

Normally we use an indefinite article (*a* or *an*) when we first refer to something generically, then on second reference we use a definite article. So you might hear, "I saw *a* dog" followed by "*The* dog was sitting quietly by a bus stop." If you hear a definite article on first reference ("I saw *the* librarian") you'll be left with questions: which librarian, has this person been mentioned before, should I know whom is meant?

However, in 2.5.1 we clearly see *the waitress*, which features a definite article on first reference to this person. Despite this, you were not left wondering which waitress was meant, unlike in the earlier case of the librarian. You have schematic knowledge of restaurants and you know that some restaurants have table service, so *the waitress* was present in the discourse once *a restaurant* was mentioned. You also assume the presence of other restaurant-related things, such as cooks, tables, food and, importantly, *the check* that must be paid after eating. You can do all of this because you're a person who knows about restaurants, or more precisely Western-style service restaurants. The producer of this text assumes you can make sense of it as a discourse by inserting all those missing elements (waitress, check, etc.) into the text yourself, thus filling in the boring bits.

Hoey (2001) argues that you may even situate this discourse somewhere in the world, perhaps seeing a name like *John* as indicating that this takes place in an English-speaking country like the United States or Britain, and seeing *hamburger* and *Coke* as being further reinforcement that this bit of action takes place somewhere that people typically eat and drink those items.

The sentences in 2.5.2 may have caused you to think a bit when reading them. The first sentence is grammatically the same, although *John* has become *Kazuhisa. His ticket* might strike you as odd, as *tickets* and *restaurants* don't have a salient lexically cohesive link for many of us. *The machine* will also probably give you pause. Your schematic knowledge of restaurants doesn't extend far enough down the hierarchy of restaurants to this particular type of restaurant.

However, if you know that customers in fast food restaurants in Japan select their food at a vending machine, pay for it there, receive a paper ticket, then hand the ticket to a server, this will be perfectly sensible to you. *Kazuhisa*, a Japanese man's name, and *gyudon*, a beef and rice dish, may signal that this series of events is happening somewhere unfamiliar to many of us, but the presence of the unexplained *the* in *the machine* is the point at which many non-Japanese tell me they can't "see" what is happening. If your schematic knowledge of restaurants doesn't include ticket machines, it is hard to create a sensible picture of what is happening in this discourse.

Note that these schematic omissions are not like the omissions that were attributed to ellipsis in Chapter 1. Missing elliptical information can be recovered from the co-text. The missing information being described here is either present or not in the discourse receiver's schematic knowledge.

For a final simple example of how schematic knowledge influences our thinking and our language use, consider this children's game my niece taught me. Ask someone to say *silk* five times quickly. Then immediately ask "What do cows drink?" It amazes me how often people, including me the first time, will respond *milk*. The answer, of course, is *water*, but the sound similarity of *silk* and *milk*, the collocation between *cow* and *milk*, and our schematic knowledge of cows' role as milk producers all seem to trick us into giving the wrong response.

Exercise – schema

Read the following excerpt from *Adventures of Huckleberry Finn* by Mark Twain. How do you, the reader of this text, turn it into a meaningful discourse based on your schematic knowledge? Point out relations between words that exist in your head, although these relations are not indicated explicitly in the text itself.

"We went tiptoeing along a path amongst the trees back towards the end of the widow's garden, stooping down so as the branches wouldn't scrape our heads. When we was passing by the kitchen I fell over a root and made a noise."

Exercise – schema (commentary)

This is the first mention of a garden in the novel, although the widow's house has been mentioned earlier, so readers have no trouble supposing the existence of a garden, assuming they are familiar with a certain type of house. Similarly, the existence of a garden allows us to imagine that there are trees and branches therein, as they are possible meronyms of garden. Our schematic knowledge helps us understand why it was necessary to stoop to avoid the branches; we know that branches can be low on trees. We can also understand why falling over a root might make noise and what kind of noise it might be. Here the details have been left out, but readers fill them in. It would strike you as silly if Twain had included the entire series of events here: "I caught my foot on a root, which caused me to lose my balance, I then fell to the ground, which caused me some pain, I signalled this pain by making a noise." Of course, the noise may have been caused by the narrator's body hitting the ground, not by him exclaiming in pain. Again, the "boring details" of Schank and Abelson (1977, p. 41) are omitted. The type of noise is not important. The noise itself is enough for the story to progress, as another character hears the noise and reacts to it.

Other linguists have introduced terms that are similar to schema in an attempt to account for this ability we have to take linguistic shortcuts when we produce a discourse, and for receivers to ignore these shortcuts and make sense of what we mean, rather than just what we say or write. Goffman (1974) called these *frames*, and suggested that we organise our experiences according to cultural or social norms. De Beaugrande used the term *global perspectives on knowledge*, which suggests that accounting for the implicit presence of widely understood information is crucial to understanding discourse.

Note – mood

In English, clauses appear largely in one of three moods: declarative, interrogative and imperative. The **declarative mood** is used to indicate things, or to "declare" them, as the name suggests. In declaratives the subject of the clause comes before the verb. (Examples 1 through 9 in this grammar note are song titles from *The Beatles*. Subjects are printed in bold, verbs are in italics.)

1. **I** *saw* her standing there.
2. **She** *came in* through the bathroom window.
3. **Happiness** *is* a warm gun.

The **interrogative mood** is used to ask questions. In interrogatives part of the verb comes before the subject. Question words (who, what, where and so on) may also appear before the subject.

4. *Do* **you** *want* to know a secret?
5. Why *don't* **we** *do* it in the road?
6. How *do* **you** *do* it?

Remember that *interrogative* is a grammatical distinction, in that part of the verb appears first, such as in "Are you hungry?" and "Would you like some lunch?" Anything can be made into a question by using rising intonation in spoken language. "Hungry?" and "Lunch?" are questions, but not interrogatives.

The **imperative mood** is used to prompt receivers to take some action. Imperatives typically begin with a verb and don't have a subject in the text.

7. *Ask* me why.
8. *Drive* my car.
9. *Don't let* me down.

The subject of an imperative will be understood as part of the discourse by considering who is being addressed. "Do not enter without authorisation" applies to anyone who doesn't have authorisation. "Come here" might apply to whomever is being looked at or pointed to by the speaker. Imperatives are sometimes called commands, but *command* may seem too forceful for many imperatives, which can often be understood as suggestions. I prefer to think of imperatives as prompts. (A more detailed discussion of grammatical mood appears in Chapter 3.)

Non-propositional meaning

Thus far, without having drawn attention to it, we have been looking at meaning and sense in declarative clauses. Declaratives are the most common type of clause in most forms of discourse as they convey information directly for the most part. We talk and write about things by choosing a subject and then a predicate that provides more information about that subject. This book is almost entirely a series of declarative clauses. In the previous sentence I chose a subject, *This book*, and I then provided more information in the predicate, *is almost entirely a series of declarative clauses*. This declarative makes a **proposition**, a claim that can be said to be true or false. Only declaratives can make these "true or false" propositions. Other types of clauses, all phrases and individual words don't make propositions as we can't say that they are true or false.

Compare the following examples, the first of which you may recognise as the first line of J. M. Barrie's *Peter Pan.*

2.6
1.   All children, except one, grow up. – declarative clause
2.   Do all children grow up? – interrogative clause
3.   Grow up – imperative clause
4.   all children – phrase
5.   children – word

Only the declarative can be said to be either true or false. We can say that children *do* grow up, or that children *do not* grow up. (Peter

Pan is the one who does not, but you can now argue about whether fictional characters should be counted in this discussion or not.) The interrogative is neither true nor false. Although the answer to the interrogative may be *yes* or *no*, and thus a proposition, the interrogative itself is not true or false. The question is asking for confirmation or denial, but no proposition has been made. The imperative is prompting its receiver to do something, but we can't say anything about whether "Grow up" is true or false. (Compare this to "He should grow up before he gets in trouble", which is a declarative and to which we can say "That's true, he should" or "That's false, he will be fine.") Neither the phrase nor the single word is a proposition. We know what *children* and *all children* mean, but nothing is proposed about them that we can say is true or false.

Declaratives have **propositional meaning**, so we can start to make sense of them from the words themselves. Barrie writes, "All children, except one, grow up" and we can agree or disagree with this and proceed from there. On the other hand, interrogatives, imperatives, phrases and individual words don't make propositions. They have **non-propositional meaning**, that is, meaning that can't be said to be true or false, and they thus often demand more thought to make sense of them when they appear in discourse. This is important for the study of discourse because while we are able to make sense of non-propositional meaning, we always have to consider the context to do so. (Much is made of propositions and their relation to meaning in books on philosophy and logic. It is beyond the scope of this book to say more than I have here, but you can read a thorough explanation of the intersection of language and logic in Brown and Yule (1983).)

Advertisements are notable for using non-propositional meaning. Advertisers who make overly strong claims about their products risk being sued by competitors or disciplined by the Advertising Standards Authority. They are thus often more tentative about describing their products. Every time you see a product advertised as being *new* or *improved* you're forced to make sense of non-propositional meaning. Is the product itself new, or are just some features of the product new? No proposition is made, so the interpretation is left to you. If the product is an existing one you will make sense of *new* as new taste, new packaging or new features, for example, depending on what product is being advertised. The phrase *improved taste* on a package of cereal is similarly ambiguous. Does this mean that the taste has been improved over competitor's products, or that it has been improved over previous versions of the same cereal? And if it is a claim of improvement over previous versions of the product, how has the taste been improved? It is now sweeter? More savoury? Saltier? This is an **implicit comparison**, which doesn't tell us what is being compared to what. (An **explicit comparison** makes clear what is being compared to what: "This package is larger than our competitor's package.") This technique is useful for advertisers as it allows them to avoid specifying what exactly has been improved, leaving it for consumers to decide.

You make sense of non-propositional meaning based on your knowledge of an advertisement's purpose, which is to sell you a product or a service. For example, the web page and some advertisements for TAG Heuer watches display the words "Swiss", "Avant-Garde" and "Since 1860". None of these is a declarative clause, so none is a proposition. We are not told directly how we should make sense of these words. As this is an advertisement, you're no doubt supposed to see this as positive information. The denotation of *Swiss* is simply "of Switzerland", but potential purchasers will also realise that *Swiss* has connotations that include reliability and tradition. The watches themselves should then be seen as reliable and traditional. *Avant-Garde* means "modern" and "experimental", qualities we are supposed to associate with the watches. Remember, the meaning is non-propositional, so it doesn't say "Our watches are avant-garde." Any association you make between the words and the watches is made because of the placement of the words and your assumption that advertising will promote positive aspects of the goods being publicised. "Since 1860" tells us that the company has been in existence for over a century and a half, so it must be reliable to have succeeded for so long. If the advertisement said "Having been in business since 1860 means we are reliable", it would be making a proposition and telling you directly what to think, but "Since 1860" demands that you participate to make sense of it.

Note that there is nothing inherently positive about "Swiss", "Avant-Garde" and "Since 1860". Some people dislike avant-garde art and music, for example, preferring traditional forms. Restaurants sometimes advertise themselves with signs saying "New owner". In this case, we are presumably supposed to ignore the fact that the company has not yet been tested and to see only the potential benefits of new ownership. As with "Since 1860", the words "New owner" are not necessarily positive in and of themselves. We are supposed to pick out the potential beneficial aspects of new ownership and disregard any detrimental ones when we make sense of this.

Exercise – non-propositional meaning

Look at the following advertising slogan. Explain how readers are supposed to make sense of it.

1. Eat Fresh – Subway

Exercise – non-propositional meaning (commentary)

Eat Fresh is an imperative, so it doesn't provide us with a proposition. (Something like "Our food is fresh" would be a proposition.) We are prompted to do something, but not told specifically how this prompt should be associated with Subway, so we must supply some of the meaning ourselves. Linking *eat* with a sandwich maker is not particularly difficult, so we are being prompted to eat Subway's food. The word *fresh* introduces positive connotations of recently picked vegetables, newly baked bread and so on. (Note that *fresh* in "fresh water" would be interpreted as "not salty", but the collocation with *eat* will push us to make sense of this differently.)

This slogan is grammatically **marked**, meaning "unusual", as *fresh* is normally an adjective, so we might expect it to appear before a noun, such as in "Eat fresh food to be healthy." The absence of an object in the slogan ("Eat Fresh *what*?") may catch readers' eyes, prompting them to supply their own "thing to be eaten". We can't be sure of exactly how Subway wants us to interpret this, and different readers will make sense of this in different ways, but forcing us to think about the interpretation of the non-propositional slogan keeps it in our minds longer than if the thinking was done for us.

Making sense in conversation

Conversations, as they were defined in Chapter 1, are spoken inter-actions among small groups of people. Spoken discourse of this type often takes places among people who are together in the same place, know something about each other and share common know-ledge. Cutting (2002, p. 56–57) calls these the situational context, the interpersonal background context and the cultural background, but I prefer the more uniform terms I use below.

The **situational context** is the physical world that surrounds the participants in the discourse. Speakers can use exophoric references (see Chapter 1) to indicate things that are present in the locale, relying on listeners to interpret them by being in the same place and using their physical senses of sight, hearing, touch, smell and taste. Saying, "Look at that" is interpretable to someone who is with you, but not to those who can't see you. (Remember that *interpretable* in this sense indicates that outsiders, those not present for the conversation, would know they were to look at something, but not precisely at what.) Par-ticipants don't have to share the same physical space, as the situational context can be extended to include each participant's location, despite being in different places. In a telephone conversation "It's so beautiful here" might refer all of Australia, for example, if the speaker was on vacation.

The **interpersonal context** is the specific shared knowledge that discourse participants have about each other and their lives. Speak-ers in conversations can take linguistic short cuts by omitting infor-mation that other participants will know because of a shared history. My wife once responded to a question about her brother by saying "Cheung is Cheung." On the surface, this appears to be needlessly repetitive. Of course *he* is *him*. However, we make sense of this by seeing that the first *Cheung* is not the same as the second *Cheung*. We take this to mean something like "Cheung [now] is Cheung [as he always is]." You would similarly understand that if I was evalu-ating my meal and said "A hamburger is a hamburger", I meant "This hamburger is like all other hamburgers. Nothing special." However, in the case of hamburgers, you can make some judgement based on having eaten one before. In the case of Cheung, you don't know him so you can't make precise sense of how he is now.

In 2.7, a father (*F*) is talking to his young daughter (*D*). The two speakers rely on interpersonal knowledge to decide how the four-year-old should wear her hair. (Note that <.> represents a short but noticeable pause of about one second.)

2.7
```
01 F: do you need your hair done
02 D: its a school day because you have your tie on
03 F: come closer then <.> I'll do it
```

In line 02, the daughter indicates that she knows she has school because her father is wearing a tie; he wears a tie to work through the week and she attends school on the same days. The father responds by saying "I'll do it", where "do it" means "put your hair in a pony-tail". Her school's regulations require her to wear her hair tied up if it is long enough to touch her shoulders. Neither of them says these extra bits of information as they talk, but their presence in the discourse is obvious to each of them as they react as if the words were said.

The **cultural context** is the shared cultural knowledge that the speakers have. *Culture* in this sense need not refer to culture at a national level: British culture, Indian culture, Brazilian culture and so on. In the social sciences, *culture* can refer to smaller groups of people with shared knowledge and social behaviours: internet culture, hip-hop culture and football culture are all possibilities. I have watched Japanese-speaking skateboarders from Tokyo communicate quite effectively with English-speaking skateboarders from Toronto, for example, based on their shared knowledge of skateboarding culture. Words like *longboard* and *freeride* made sense to them, but not to me. (How "long" is a longboard, for example? They knew, but I did not.)

In 2.8, a university lecturer responds to a student's question about an essay due date by assuming shared cultural knowledge.

2.8
```
01 student:  is that due on december 20
02 lecturer: no because that's christmas
03 student:  so it must be the week before
```

Here the reason given in line 02, "that's Christmas", is obviously enough for the student to understand, but quite a bit of shared cultural context is assumed by the lecturer. Shared knowledge of holy days (Christmas is important to Christians), bank holidays (many people don't work on Christmas day, not only Christians) and British university culture (many British universities close for two weeks around Christmas, essays are not submitted when the university is closed) are all relevant to making sense of the lecturer's response.

Cultural context knowledge overlaps to an extent with the schematic knowledge described earlier in this chapter, but they are not precisely the same. If I told you that *Chuseok* was a holiday in Korea you would have some schematic knowledge of holidays based on your own experiences, but no cultural context knowledge of the importance of *Chuseok*, unless of course you're Korean.

I referred to these three concepts (situational, interpersonal and cultural context) as being particularly important in spoken conversation, but their presence can be noted in other forms of discourse. However, the genre of discourse will often preclude a reliance on some forms of shared knowledge. For example, in this book I can't assume any shared situational context, as I don't know where you will be reading it. I can use endophoric "in-text" references, but not exophoric references to the place in which you're sitting or standing at the moment. I can't assume much shared interpersonal knowledge, either. The only things we know about each other are those things I have told you about myself. This text is unidirectional, going from me to you. On the other hand, I can assume a certain amount of shared cultural context. This book is aimed at an audience of British university students. (Note that *British* here means the university is British, not that you're necessarily British, which is an important distinction in terms of how much shared cultural knowledge I can assume.) The assumptions I make about shared cultural context knowledge are based on that, so when I mention holidays, I can, for example, assume that you do know about *Christmas* even if you're not a Christian, but not about *Chuseok*.

In other cases, a speech by a public figure might refer to situational context and cultural context, but make little reference to interpersonal context; the listeners may know the speaker, but the speaker won't know all of them. An email exchange between employees at different branches of a company could include cultural context (the company's policies and procedures would be shared knowledge), although the employees might not know each other personally and could not see or hear what was happening in each other's situational context.

Exercise – discourse in context

In the following excerpt of a conversation, a grandmother (*GM*) and a grandfather (*GF*) in one location are talking to their granddaughter (*D*) who is in another location. They are using Skype, a video-calling service, so they can only see whatever is positioned directly in front of the other person's laptop camera. (Note that <.> represents a pause of about one second, while <..> represents a pause of about two seconds.)

```
01 GM: move that move that left or maybe your right so I can see
02     it <.> I am never sure which way to say
03 D:  can you see ⁄it <..> I made it at school at art club
04 GM: oh it's wonderful did you make it at school
05 D:  at art club
06 GM: oh yes it's today that your daddy picks you up
07 GF: if you stop moving we can see better <..> there it is
08 GM: is it someone from Rainbow Magic
09 D:  fairies have wings
10 GM: oh of course they have wings <.> you're not so interested
11     in that anymore
```

Exercise – discourse in context (commentary)

In line 01, "that" is interpretable to the participants because the child is holding a painting. Outsiders, those like us who were not part of the conversation, can't interpret "that" since we were not part of the situational context. (We can go back and guess what "that" is once we have read the entire transcript, but we can't be sure in line 01.) References to "it" (lines 03, 04 and 07) are similarly dependent on knowing the situational context. Line 06's sense ("it's today") is partly dependent on knowing the interpersonal context. The child attends art club after school one day per week, after which her father collects her, instead of her mother as is usual on the other days. *GM* makes this explicit in line 06. Lines 08, 09 and 10 rely on quite specific knowledge of *Rainbow Magic*, a series of children's books about fairies. *GM* (line 08) asks if the painting is a character from the series of fairy books. *D*'s turn in line 09 says "fairies have wings", but is made sense of as "because fairies have wings, this can't be a fairy as the figure in the picture doesn't have wings". *GM* acknowledges this in line 10 ("oh of course") and then shows an awareness of interpersonal context by commenting that the child is "not so interested in that [*Rainbow Magic*] anymore". As you read this extract you will have understood much of what was being discussed, but your sense-making ability may have been tested in some places. This is to be expected, as the conversation was not designed with you in mind, but was designed for the participants in a specific place with specific knowledge about each other and the world.

Chapter 3

Thinking about the Producer

In this chapter we look at *variation*, which is the description of how people use language differently depending on various social factors (age, gender, ethnicity, class and geographical origin). People who speak or write in recognisably similar ways are said to use a *variety* of English. We also look at a tool for accurately describing how producers relate to their receivers by telling them, asking them or prompting them with language.

In a famous scene from the *Star Wars* series of films, the primary villain, Darth Vader, is battling with the hero, Luke Skywalker. Darth Vader, an intimidating black-costumed figure, surprises the film's audience when he says, "I am your father", shocking Luke, who had previously thought his father was a dead hero. This revelation, combined with Vader's deep voice, has made this a memorable quotation from the film.

Imagine that instead of saying "I am your father", Vader had said, "I'm your dad." Suddenly the words, which mean the same thing, sound comical. Partly this is because the expanded form *I am* has become the contraction *I'm*. We tend to expect contractions like *I'm* in informal situations, not during a serious battle in which Vader has already cut off Luke's arm. More noticeably, *father* has become *dad*. Both words mean the same thing, but have different connotations. *Father* is relatively neutral, but *dad* conjures up images of close family relations. (Consider how we use the word *offspring* for baby animals but *children* for human babies for another example of how words that essentially denote the same thing can have different connotations. I think many people would be offended if you referred to their children as their *offspring*.)

Having Darth Vader talk in a certain way is part of how the film portrays his character. We can see his clothes and actions, which tell us a certain amount about what type of character he is, but his words give us the most information. He does not use informal, friendly words like *dad* because he is distant and cold.

Darth Vader is a fictional character, but we can think about how words portray real people in a similar way. Goffman's (1959) book *The Presentation of Self in Everyday Life* drew an analogy between actors playing characters, who are distinguished by their props, clothes and lines, and real people, who portray themselves according to how they dress, act and use language. Semioticians and students of fashion may be interested in the clothes and props people display; linguists are interested in the words.

Everyone produces language in different ways, both when speaking and when writing. Do you call the roundish red thing that is used in many pasta sauces a *to-MAY-to* or a *to-MAH-to*? Do you call a tomato a *fruit*, as botanists do because of its biological properties, or do you call it a *vegetable*, as many chefs do because of the way it is used in cooking? Is that long green vegetable that you might eat with a tomato called a *courgette* or a *zucchini*? Think of your choices in these cases, and in all the others you make as you speak, as being your lines in a play. They tell your listeners something about you as a person.

Crystal (2008), in an overview of his own and other scholars' research, estimates that almost two billion people in the world speak English. This number, which includes native speakers and others for whom English is a second or additional language, makes English the most widely spoken language in the world. (Mandarin Chinese has the most native speakers, but not near as many second language speakers.)

In theory, none of these speakers of English uses the language the same way as any other speaker. Each has his or her own **idiolect**, a unique way of speaking that marks him or her as distinct from everyone else. You may have a sister or brother, perhaps even a twin, raised in the same home as you by the same parents. Despite this, he reads science fiction novels while you watch comedies on television. She likes football while you play hockey. These experiences, plus all of the others that are part of your life, will have contributed to the stock of words that you tend to use.

Idiolect is a term that is related to **dialect**, the speech habits "characteristic of a geographical area or region, or of a specific social group" (Swann *et al.*, 2004, p. 76). (Note that **accent**, which Hughes *et al.* (2005, p. 2) define as "variations in pronunciation", is not the same as "dialect". "Accent" refers only to pronunciation and intonation, while "dialect" includes accent, grammar and vocabulary.)

You and your siblings, parents and others from your neighbourhood may use the same dialect, so you have similar accents and use similar local words and slang, but you differ enough that no two of you are exactly the same. I wrote that idiolect is a concept that exists "in theory" above, because while the evidence appears to favour the conclusion that we are each linguistically distinct, it is in practice impossible to test this conclusion. How could we gather data from each of those almost two billion English speakers? Nevertheless, it is almost immediately evident when you hear two people speak that there are noticeable differences between them.

You'll notice that people's voices differ by **pitch**, as some of us have higher voices and others have lower voices. You'll also notice that people's voices differ by **timbre**, the difference in the qualities of the sound of a person's voice. (It is differences in timbre that allow us to recognise the difference between a saxophone, a piano and a guitar, even if all three instruments were to play a note of the same pitch.) When someone calls you on the phone and you recognise his or her voice from "Hello", you're recognising his or her pitch and timbre.

Pitch and timbre are largely physical properties of the voice. Unless you're trying to disguise yourself, you likely don't make a conscious choice about these two characteristics of your voice. There are, however, numerous other features of your speech production that you do make choices about, albeit likely very quickly as you're talking. Which words do you use? Which grammatical choices do you make? How formal or informal are you?

I have been referring to spoken language over the last few paragraphs, as we often find it easier to detect differences in the way people speak, but the same principles apply to written language. When critics refer to an *author's voice* they are pointing out that different writers, especially those who are highly proficient at writing, are often distinguishable in terms of the linguistic choices they make when they write.

Not only does each of us use language, both spoken and written, differently from everyone else, but we each use language differently at different times. This is neatly summarised in the distinction between language *user* and language *use*. Different *users* of language produce language in different ways based on certain **social variables** (Swann *et al*., 2004): age, gender, ethnicity, class and geographical origin. Linguistic variation is also caused by differing language *use*: the topic of the discourse, the purpose of the discourse, whether the discourse is written or spoken and so on. (Language use-based variation, also known as **register**, is discussed in Chapter 4.)

As a language *user* I'm defined by my age (44 years old as I write this), my gender (male) and my geographical origin (Canadian), among other variables. These are those variables which don't change, or do so only slowly. My age obviously changes year-by-year, but perhaps less obviously my Canadian English has also changed after having lived in England for almost a decade. When once I said *elevator* I now say *lift*, for example, or at least I do when I'm in the United Kingdom.

My linguistic variation based on language *use*, however, changes rapidly. When I talk in class, I speak more formally than when I meet my students in my office. When I speak with students of linguistics at university I use words like *phonology* and *syntax*, but when children at my daughter's primary school ask about my job I use phrases like *sounds of English* and *rules of English*. When I chat with my boss in the hallway, I call her by her first name, but if I write her an official email about some aspect of work, I address her by her title, "professor", and her family name. Each time I use language I make judgements about what I'm talking about, to whom and for what purpose.

Sociolinguistics and language variation according to *user*

In black-and-white Western films and television programmes, the heroes typically wore white hats and the villains wore black hats. This made them easily distinguishable among crowds of cowboys, especially on the small television screens of the black-and-white era. (For the same reason sports teams had two uniforms, one dark and one light, to avoid confusion.) We may now find such sartorial divisions quaint in an era of large, high-definition colour screens, but more recent films do consistently use language variation to signify whether characters are heroes or villains.

In American-made Hollywood films there is a significant trend for villains to have British, usually English, accents: numerous *Star Wars* villains, Magneto in the *X-Men* films, Alan Rickman's characters in *Robin Hood* and *Die Hard*, the evil prince in *Shrek* (an American actor using a faux-British accent), the evil humans in *Fantastic Mr Fox*, most of the wicked stepmothers and evil queens in Disney films and so on. Notably, the heroes of many of these films (*Shrek, Star Wars, Fantastic Mr Fox*) have American accents, which makes these heroes aurally distinct from the villains. Whether this "British accents for villains" trope is a sign of American attitudes to Britain or whether it is simply because Britain is the second-most populous English-speaking country, and thus produces many actors, is a matter for others to decide. Either way, there is no question that accents help us distinguish between people.

In the play *Pygmalion*, Shaw wrote "It is impossible for an Englishman to open his mouth without making some other Englishman hate or despise him." Although this was an overstatement for comic effect, Shaw was correctly pointing out that we make judgements about people based on how they talk. If you met me in London, England, and you heard me talk, you would know I was not a locally born person because of my accent. Depending on how familiar you are with accents you would perhaps guess that I am North American, and if you were even more attuned to accents, you could place me as Canadian. On the other hand, if you met me in London, Canada, where my accent is quite common, you would probably judge that I was a local.

Dunbar (2004, p. 106) argues that **internal variation**, meaning differences in the way we each use the same language, may have evolved as a way of allowing us to identify those who are not from the same place as us. "Because they are difficult to acquire if they are not learned early in life, dialects allow community members to identify those who are likely to share a common history of obligation (and hence to be trustworthy reciprocators)." According to this reasoning, in the past, before the police protected us from criminals, before official identification cards allowed us to prove who we were, differences in the ways people spoke the same language allowed listeners to identify those who were not local, and who therefore might not be as trustworthy as those from the immediate locale.

Phonological variation

Sociolinguists look at three aspects of variation when they describe what it is that makes a person's language distinct. The first, **phonological variation**, is the most noticeable variable in spoken language. (It is not noticeable at all in written language, of course, just as variations in spelling are not noticeable in spoken language.) The word *batter*, for example, can be realised in numerous ways. Considering only the *tt* consonant in the middle of the word, we can hear it pronounced "batter" in much of Britain, but "badder" in much of North America. In careful speech North Americans might pronounce it "batter", but in common practice the *tt* is realised as a *d* sound, so "badder".

The *tt* in *batter* is called a **linguistic variable**, which means it is something that can be realised in more than one way. The realisation a speaker uses, whether a *t* sound in "batter" or *d* sound in "badder", is called a **linguistic variant**. The *variable* is what might happen; the *variant* is what happens in the specific case you're analysing. In the case of *medicine*, the first *i* is a phonological variable, so North Americans typically realise the word as "med-i-cine", pronouncing the *i*, while British people realise it as "med-cine", omitting the *i* sound entirely. Returning to *batter*, there is at least one other linguistic variable in the word that affects its final realisation. People in Britain are more likely to pronounce the *er* at the end of *batter* as "ah", while North Americans tend to say "er." So *er* is the variable, and the variant is either "ah" or "er", whichever is actually spoken. It is important to remember that linguistic variants are those differences which change the sound of the word, but don't change the meaning. *Butter* is not a variant of *batter*; it is a different word.

This means the whole word *batter* has at least two possible realisations: "badder" and "battah". Which of these is correct? From a linguistic point of view both of them are. This is not a cop out linguists use to avoid commenting on what, for some, is a contentious issue. Instead, linguists are thinking about language as having two main functions: a communicative function and a social function. The **communicative function** of language refers to what people may commonly think of when they discuss the purpose of language; we use language to talk or write about actions, thoughts, emotions and so on. (A detailed list of the things we talk and write about is given in the explanation of the ideational metafunction in Chapter 2.) The **social function** of language refers to the idea that as we produce language we constantly provide receivers with information about our social selves. When a British person says "battah", he communicates information about that thing, *batter*, but he also provides social information about who he is, which in this case is British. When an American says "badder", she communicates the same thing, but provides social information, which says "I'm American" at the same time. (By referring to American and British people here I'm simplifying the concepts, because of course when we hear people from other countries we may also notice something about where they may be from.)

Both realisations of *batter* are communicatively the same, so with more co-text you would know whether the person means "a mixture for making cake", "a person with a bat" or "to hit something repeatedly." None of these phonological realisations is meant to change the communicative meaning of the word, but each realisation does express social information about the language user who says it.

National origin, whether British, American, Australian, etc., is not the only source of phonological variation. Radford *et al.* (2009) provide an example of how class difference can correlate with variation in the way people realise the *h* sound at the beginning of a word like *hammer*. In general, working-class people pronounced the word as "ammer", preferring a variant where the *h* was not realised at all, while middle-class people preferred "hammer", making the *h* audible. Gender can also correlate with phonological variation, with boys and men being more likely to realise the *ing* in words like *walking* as "walkin" and women and girls showing a higher preference for "walking".

It is very important to point out that variation is rarely absolute, meaning that we can't say that "all British people do this", "100 per cent of working class people do that" and so on. We can notice trends and can make some predictions based on those trends, but can't be certain what someone will do until we hear him or her speak.

Exercise – phonological variation

Make a list of three or four words that you pronounce differently from other people. Compare yourself to people you know or people on television and the radio. Identify what part(s) of the words are phonological variables and what the possible variants are. Identify who uses each variant: are they from a different country, or from a different region of your country, are they younger or older than you?

Next, think about whether one of the variants is generally considered "better" than the other by most people. Is there one variant that people say "sounds funny"? Is one of them associated with being uneducated or educated, or with being lazy?

Exercise – phonological variation (commentary)

Your answers to the first part of this exercise will vary depending on the words you chose. For example, North Americans and British people generally realise the word *can* in a similar manner, but pronounce *can't* quite differently from each other. The "a" vowel in *can't* is a phonological variable that is realised as a different variant depending on whether you speak North American English or British English. (As always, I am simplifying here, because there is variation within North America and within Britain as well.)

Your answer to the second part of the exercise, concerning which variant is "better", may have led you to think about **linguistic prejudice**, the negative attitudes some may have towards certain accents. For example, in some places in England the *tt* in *batter* is not pronounced at all, which leads to a realisation that sounds like "ba-er". In linguistics this is typically written as *ba?er*, where the ? represents a **glottal stop**, in which the speaker's *glottis*, part of the larynx, stops air from coming out for a brief moment.

A glottal stop in *batter* is sometimes frowned upon, with users of that variant being accused of linguistic laziness or sloppiness. From a linguistic point of view, the glottal stop is perfectly communicative. Even if you don't use it, once you've heard it a couple of times you'll have no trouble recognising it and understanding that *ba?er* means "batter". Linguists tend to be quite liberal about variants like this. However, linguists aren't stupid. They know that some people, those who think language should be realised in certain ways and not others, will dislike this glottal stop. The glottal stop may be seen as uncommunicative or socially undesirable. Someone who uses this glottal stop may not get hired for a job, for example, if the recruiter thinks it is a sign of an inferior intellect.

Interestingly, hearing a glottal stop in words like *batter* or *little* ("li?le") may seem marked to you, but in other words most English speakers use glottal stops. Many of us only pronounce the *t* in *curtain* or the *tt* in *button* in careful speech, realising those words as "cur?ain" and "bu?on" instead. However, we are not stigmatised for using glottal stops in those places, as it is common for most people to do so. So it isn't the glottal stop itself that is significant, but rather where they are realised.

Lexical variation

Once you have understood the concepts of *variable* (acceptable possibilities) and *variant* (the possibility that is realised), you will see that they can also be applied to *lexical variation*, differences in word meaning. The following exchange, between detective Hercule Poirot and a man named Blondin, appears in Agatha Christie's *Death on the Nile*, first published in 1937.

"I am, hélas, a man of leisure," he said sadly. "I have made the economies in my time and I have now the means to enjoy a life of idleness."

"I envy you."

"No, no, you would be unwise to do so. I can assure you, it is not so gay as it sounds."

What does Poirot mean by *gay*? The word *gay* in Friedrich Nietzsche's *The Gay Science*, which was first published in 1882, meant "happy", and the phrase "the gay science" was known at the time to mean "poetry". Readers of Christie's novel at the time it was published would have understood *gay* in a similar sense. The theme song from the 1960s animated television series *The Flintstones* ended with the line "We'll have a gay old time", where again *gay* was realised in the sense of "happy".

By the time I was a young student in the 1980s, *gay* was used to mean "homosexual", so I recall being confused by *gay* in *The Flintstones* song. *Gay* had begun to mean "homosexual" some time before that, co-existing with the sense "happy", but by the 1980s the "homosexual" variant was more common. The word in the song did not seem to be consistent with what I heard in the schoolyard. Here the possible meaning of the word *gay* is the variable, while the sense of the word *gay* that is meant in the discourse being analysed is the variant. I remember reading letters in the newspaper in which people argued that *gay* meant "happy" and shouldn't be used to mean "homosexual", but that argument has largely been lost and the "homosexual" variant is the more common current meaning of *gay*. We now typically only encounter *gay* in the sense of "happy" in older texts, which shows us how lexical variation is sometimes a useful tool for helping identify discourse as a product of a certain time. (You'll recognise the *gay* "happy" variant if you've ever heard the Christmas song *Deck the Halls*, which includes the line "Don we now our gay apparel".)

Phonological variation also occurs over time, so for example the silent *k* in *knife* and *knight* used to be pronounced, but we don't have many recordings of speech from the past, so most of us are not familiar with how English used to sound. (The oldest English language recordings are from the late nineteenth century, but they are few and far between.) Lexical variation is easier to see, as we can more readily access old written texts.

Major language changes tend to take the shape of an s-curve, meaning that at first very few people use the new variant, then there is a rapid uptake of the variant by most users of the language. Eventually, those few people who preferred not to use the newer variant either start doing so or die, leaving the previous variant to exist only in older texts. This process is similar to the process by which people start using new technologies. At first only technological "early adopters" bought smart phones. Once the phones showed themselves to be useful, masses of people bought them.

As with differences in phonological variation, most linguists would hesitate before saying that one meaning of *gay*, or any other word, is correct. This is because many researchers in the field practise **descriptive linguistics**, meaning they aim to describe what language users do and why, without making judgements about what is correct or not. *Gay* meaning "happy" is correct in those discourses in which it was used in the past and *gay* more recently is correct when it means "homosexual"; that is the extent of a brief descriptive account of the use of that word. **Prescriptive linguistics**, on the other hand, attempts to rationalise why language should be used in certain ways. When language teachers tell you to "say it like this", they are being prescriptive, as are government policies that set schooling regulations. ("Weird Al" Yankovic's song *Word Crimes* manages to list dozens of prescriptivist bugbears, such as the difference between *less* and *fewer*, in a four-minute song. It's well worth listening to, or better yet watching, if you want to catch all the references.) Those letter-writers I mentioned earlier were attempting to prescribe the correct use of *gay*, as they saw it.

People who use dictionaries in an attempt to argue about correct uses of language have misunderstood the difference between description and prescription, I think. Dictionaries are descriptions of language use; they tell us what people do, but not what people should do. Lexicographers, the people who create dictionaries, read and listen to language, watching for new variants of word meanings. They **attest** new words and new variants, meaning they watch for them to be used in reputable sources and in ways that allows them to be understood. When a new variant meaning has been attested enough times, it may be entered in the dictionary. So the new word or variant only enters the dictionary after it is already being used by enough people for it to be noticeable. The dictionary describes what people do, not what they should do. If this were not true, then dictionaries now would be largely the same as they were in the past, but language changes and so do our records of it.

Lexical variation does not only occur over time, as in the case of *gay*. We can see variant meanings of the same word used in different places or by different groups of speakers as well. Pavement is usually used to mean "the place to walk beside the road" in British English, but in North America it means "the material used to cover the surface of the road". Telling someone to "walk on the pavement" is therefore quite different depending on who says it. In one place you're being advised to be safe, in the other you're being told to risk your life. In the legal community a *suit* may mean "an attempt to settle a dispute in a court". In the "rag district" of London, where there are many tailors and wholesale clothiers, *suit* might be expected to more commonly refer to men's clothing.

Exercise – lexical variation

After the comedian Ricky Gervais used the word *mong* on a social media site, some people were angry with him, arguing that the word should be avoided as it was often used to disparage people with Down's Syndrome. Gervais posted these comments, among others, to defend himself:

"Well done everyone who pointed out that Mong USED to be a derogatory term for DS [Down's syndrome] Gay USED to mean happy. Words change. Get over it."
"What is a mong? A div, a dozy spud headed twonk. I would NEVER use it to mean downs syndrome."

In linguistic terms, what is the variable and what are the variants that Gervais described in his posts? Why is a word like this potentially controversial, while other words with variant meanings are not?

Exercise – lexical variation (commentary)

The linguistic variable being discussed is *mong*. The variants are the possible meanings of the word: either it is a derogatory term for Down's Syndrome or it is a negative epithet meaning something like "idiot", but that has no relation to Down's Syndrome.

As Gervais points out, "words change". This is often uncontroversial. In Middle English *girl* meant "a child of either sex", while now it means only "female child". As the "either sex" variant is now lost except in historical texts, this causes little confusion. *Presently* means both "now" and "soon". Dictionaries provide both definitions, and although some prescriptivists dislike the "now" variant, they certainly understand it. If you don't recognise that *presently* can mean "soon", you may be confused by some older texts, but you're unlikely to react emotionally to the difference.

Words like *mong* are obviously different. The newer "idiot" variant may be understood by some, but it has not replaced the older variant completely in current usage, unlike with *girl*. While the two are in use at once, it is often ambiguous to listeners which variant is meant. As Gervais' critics pointed out, the *mong* variant meaning "idiot" draws on a history of disparagement of people with Down's Syndrome to mean what Gervais says it does, and so the term should be avoided in any sense.

A similar example can be seen with racist terms. Shortening *British* to *Brit* is uncontroversial. This is known as **clipping**, producing a new word by truncating another one. Sometimes this is well-accepted, as in *laboratory* being clipped to produce *lab*. Other times, such as with *brilliant* being clipped to *brill* by some young British people, it produces a word that will only be used as slang by particular groups of people. Clipping *Pakistani* to *Paki*, while similar in terms of the word's formation, is very controversial.

Prince Harry was criticised when a video was released of him calling a British Asian soldier "our little Paki friend". He was defended by some who claimed that the word was simply a short form of *Pakistani*. Others, those who acknowledge that words exist as parts of discourse, argued that *Paki* is not simply a lexical variant meaning "Pakistani", but is more correctly seen as a variant that exists in a context where it has been used to denigrate, insult and humiliate Pakistani people. Those who use words like *mong* and *Paki* while pretending that these words don't exist as products of discourse are being disingenuous.

Grammatical variation

The final type of variation, grammatical variation, includes both syntactic and morphological variation, as grammar includes both syntax and morphology. Syntax is the study of the arrangement of words in a language; so English syntax allows "He saw them" but generally does not allow *"Saw them he." (Note that * is often used to denote a word combination that is either impossible or highly unusual. Linguists tend to shy away from saying "impossible", because as soon as one says a word order is impossible, another will go to great lengths to figure out a way that it is possible.)

Morphology is the study of how words change when they are used differently, so *teaches, taught, teacher* and *teaching* are some of the morphological forms of *teach*. *Morph* means "change" and *ology* means "study of", so *morphology* is "the study of change". (I remember this by recalling the *Mighty Morphin Power Rangers*, a children's TV programme about teenagers who could change into superheroes.)

Grammatical variation is perhaps less noticeable than phonological and lexical variation. You may hear phonological variation in almost every word that is realised with an unfamiliar accent. You may notice lexical variation when you notice new words or words that are used in ways that are different than what you're accustomed to. When it comes to grammar, variation is possible, but less common. In parts of England you may hear people say "I've had my picture took", which is a variant of the more common "I've had my picture taken." *Took* may be "wrong" according to grammar textbooks for English learners, but in a descriptive account a linguist would point out that as long as *took* is used consistently in that way, it is a regular pattern, and so is a variant, not an error.

Note – morphemes

A **morpheme** is the smallest unit of language that contains meaning. The word *walked* is made up of two morphemes: *walk* and *ed*. *Walk* gives us the basic meaning, "to travel on foot", while *ed* tells us that this was done in the past. *Walk* is a **free morpheme**, meaning it can be used on its own, as in "I walk to work most days." On the other hand, *ed* is a **bound morpheme**, as we can't use it on its own. When it tells us that something was done in the past, it always appears with at least one other morpheme: *happened* (happen + ed), *placed* (place + ed, but we eliminate one *e* when we join the two morphemes together), and *reworked* (re + work + ed).

Using morphemes like *ed* to change the grammatical form of a word is called **inflection**. When we make a plural form we typically inflect with *s*, as in *habit – habits*. We also use *s* to inflect for third person singular present simple verbs, as in *I walk – you walk – she* *walks*, and to inflect for possession, as in *the child's toy* and *Rubik's Cube*. While these three *s* bound morphemes all look the same, that is, they are all realised with *s*, it is important to remember that they are different morphemes as they inflect to provide different information.

Standard English and varieties of English

If we want to consider linguistic variation when we analyse discourse, which is the purpose of this book, we should first consider standard English. Although this term is used with various meanings in common parlance, linguists have aimed to provide a more precise definition. Trudgill (2002, p. 160) suggests that **standard English** is, among other things, "the variety of English normally used in writing, especially printing" and is "the variety spoken by those who are often referred to as 'educated people'".

There are three key points to notice here. First, in linguistic terms, standard English is a variety. It is not, as some erroneously claim, the proper language from which all others varieties deviate. It is rather one variety of English, albeit the most important variety in terms of the social power it projects when it is used. People who use standard English are often thought to be better speakers of English than those who don't, but in linguistic terms there is nothing communicatively "better" about standard English when it is compared to other varieties.

Second, standard English is normally discussed by linguists in its written form. If you compare the language used in newspapers as far apart as the *Los Angeles Times*, the *New York Times*, *The Times* of London and the *Straits Times* of Singapore, you will see little variation in the language used. Trudgill called this "printing", but perhaps it is best to think of this as the *published* form of the language variety. People write letters, emails and text messages in various ways, but these are not usually for publication. Publications that do feature other, non-standard, varieties of English are so rare as to be newsworthy when they succeed. Irvine Welsh's *Trainspotting*, a success both as a novel and as a film, perplexed some readers with stretches of text like "defines us mair accurately", in which *mair* ("more") was written to approximate the sound of the Scots English it was meant to represent. (The film version of the story, although in English, was considered to be so different from what world audiences would be used to that subtitles were sometimes used, even in English-speaking countries.)

Finally, Trudgill says standard English is the variety spoken by "educated people". He puts this phrase in quotation marks, I think, to highlight what he knows is the ambiguity inherent in this term. (How much education does one need to be "educated"? What type of education leads to proficiency in standard English?) Nevertheless, standard English is associated with education, although the term is only loosely possible to define. (Note that standard English is not usually associated with any particular accent. It is the adherence to standard lexis, grammar and morphology that makes one's language standard. You can speak English with a Glaswegian, Liverpudlian, Torontonian or Bostonian accent.)

Although standard English is not considered better than other varieties of English in linguistic terms, the association of standard English with education and publication has led to it being sometimes considered more accurate and more communicative. Those who don't use standard English are sometimes claimed to be intellectually weak, lazy speakers of English. Their language, despite being communicatively equal in real terms, is socially marked as inferior.

In 1996 a school district in Oakland, California, passed a resolution declaring that Ebonics, the variety of English spoken by many African-American students in the area, should be officially recognised. (Although the term *Ebonics* was used at the time, this is now more commonly known as African-American Vernacular English.) This move might have given the school district access to extra funding that was sometimes granted to school districts with large numbers of bilingual students. The additional funds could then have been used to help students improve their standard English. As McArthur (1998, p. 198) explains, this led to "polarization and outrage". Supporters of official recognition of Ebonics felt it would legitimise the variety, giving those who speak it an increased sense of pride, just as those who speak other varieties and languages are often proud of their linguistic abilities. Opponents of the move decried it as a nonsense, arguing that standard English was the only "credible, viable and desirable English" (McArthur, 1998, p. 200). For them, there was no value associated with non-standard English, meaning it should have no official recognition by the school system.

Exercise – standard English

A London school made news for banning its students from using words such as *coz*, *ain't*, *like*, *innit* and *bare*. Identify the communicative function of these words, then consider why a school's staff would prefer that students not use them.

1. Wear a jacket *coz* it's cold.
2. There *ain't* no reason to be worried about that.
3. She was *like* 25 years old at the time.
4. Worse time for it to happen, *innit*?
5. We've got *bare* money left, even after this.

Exercise – standard English (commentary)

Coz is being used in place of *because*, through the process of clipping discussed earlier. *Ain't* is a variant of *isn't*. *Like*, when used in this manner, is a discourse marker that indicates that the speaker may be using the words that follow imprecisely. (A **discourse marker**, as the name implies, marks the nearby discourse to show something about the speaker's attitude towards it. When you hear that someone is "like, 25 years old", you would not be surprised to find out that she is, in fact, 24. See Chapter 5 for more on discourse markers.) *Innit* is an invariant tag question, which can replace almost any tag question such as *isn't it*, *aren't they* or *don't we* at the end of a sentence. *Bare*, in this sense, means "much" or "a lot of".

These words, once you know them, have equal communicative power as their standard English equivalents. For example, it doesn't matter if you've never heard *bare* before. Once you know it, you know that "There are bare cars in the lot" means there are many cars there. Some of these words are, in reality, more communicatively effective in some ways than their standard English variants. We are typically told not to use *ain't* in a sentence like 2 above because two negatives make a positive. This may be true in mathematics, where $-2 \times -3 = 6$, but language is not mathematics. Someone who says

"There ain't no reason to be worried" is using two negatives, *ain't* and *no*, but he is not saying you should worry, but instead is emphasising the lack of need for worry. American blues musician Johnny Winter's song *Ain't Nothing to Me* relies on our knowledge of this emphatic use of *ain't* and another negative to show his complete impartiality in the affair he sings about.

The problem with *bare*, *ain't* and the other examples aren't that we don't know what they mean. We often encounter new words. If a biologist explained that *phylogenetics* was "the study of relations between different living things", people who didn't know that word would be unlikely to think it was incorrect English. The prestige of the person's job – biologists are generally thought to be intelligent – would convince listeners that the word, although rare, was standard English. The problem with words like *bare* is, rather, that for many people *bare* is non-standard, communicatively weak, English because of who uses the word. It is associated with young, urban, working-class students, not with biologists.

School teachers certainly understand the non-standard English words their young charges use, and they know their students are intelligent, but in an effort to promote their use of socially correct language they discourage the use of non-standard variants.

Language and identity

When you're analysing discourse it is productive to not only think about how different people's language use varies, but also what this variation might mean about those people in terms of how they see themselves and in terms of how others perceive them. Consider that, despite the fact that we could all speak English the same way since there is nothing physically preventing us from doing so, we don't.

For example, over the years Canadian commentators have sometimes worried that Canadians will inevitably end up sounding identical to Americans because America is a dominant producer of mass culture. Canadians hear American music and watch American television on broadcasts from American stations that reach across the border. Although American television has been showing in Canada for decades, Canadians still sound recognisably Canadian, use recognisably Canadian words and spell those words more like British people than Americans. Canadians in Toronto sound more similar to Canadians in Vancouver, a car journey of over 4,000 kilometres, than they do to Americans in Buffalo, New York, a mere 150 kilometres away. The film *South Park: Bigger Longer & Uncut* lampooned the Canadian accent, in particular the Canadian realisation of *ou* in words like *about*, which Americans hear as "a-boot". Despite the general hilarity with which the film and its mocking of Canadians' accents was received, it is unlikely that any Canadians changed their pronunciation as a result.

More seriously than *South Park*'s gentle teasing, speakers' internal variation can lead to highly negative perceptions from outsiders. Coupland & Bishop (2007), for example, found that in Britain a Birmingham accent was rated very poorly in terms of its social attractiveness and its prestige. In other words, people who spoke with that accent were thought to be both less friendly and approachable, and less educated and less likely to hold positions of power, than those who spoke with other accents. (In the United States the English spoken by many in the southern states is similarly sometimes thought to be a sign of poor education, even though former presidents Jimmy Carter and Bill Clinton spoke with noticeably southern accents.)

Why don't those with a Birmingham accent simply change the way they talk? They know their way of using English is sometimes negatively rated. They've heard jokes about it, read accounts of how it sounds uneducated and endured well-meaning attempts to convince them to speak "properly". The same could be said of others whose language is marginalised and denigrated: young people, members of ethnic minorities (whose speakers are sometimes characterised by distinct **ethnolects**), rural people and so on.

Labov (2006) argued that we should consider such rejection of standard English as a form of **covert prestige**, taking pride in being different by consciously choosing to adopt and maintain the speech norms of a group of people while knowing that those norms are often negatively rated. Singaporean politicians have criticised Singaporean people's use of Singlish, a low prestige form of English spoken in Singapore. Even Singaporeans who are **bi-dialectical**, proficient in both standard Singaporean English and Singlish, may choose to speak Singlish as an immediate marker of the fact that they are Singaporean. Their use of Singlish marks them as members of a Singaporean in-group, members of a social group with shared identity, culture and interests, while simultaneously drawing a line between themselves and those who don't speak Singlish, members of the out-group. (For example, to *arrow* in Singlish means "to order someone to do an unpleasant job". If you don't understand that when you hear it you're immediately marked as an out-group member.)

On the other hand, **overt prestige** is defined as what we might normally think of as *prestige* in its common usage. This is the prestige associated with the language of the socially powerful upper classes, that is, standard English. If you have a job interview or give a speech and you make an attempt to be on your best linguistic behaviour, you're drawing on the overt prestige of standard English.

Those who display covert prestige in their language use are choosing to show linguistic allegiance to their in-group as a marker of identity, ignoring, as Labov (2006) pointed out, the fact they know they will be mocked for speaking in such a manner. I like to think of this as a form of linguistic rebellion. People learn much of their linguistic behaviour from those they know, love and respect: their parents, their siblings, other close family members and friends. The reaction to becoming aware of the fact that these people, one's most intimate in-group, speak a variety of English that is poorly rated in terms of prestige is understandable. Reject the out-group norms of standard English and favour the in-group norms of one's more immediate social circle.

Different **speech communities**, people who are united by common linguistic variation and common speech habits, may tend to display different levels of covert and overt prestige. Typical middle-class Canadians, who as a rule are not a particularly marginalised group, may groan at yet another American joke about the Canadian accent, but don't tend to display covert prestige in their language use. Similarly, Canadians don't take offense at others who use Canadian variants as part of their language behaviour, whether in admiration or to tease.

On the other hand, working-class African Americans, a historically marginalised speech community, sometimes use African-American Vernacular English (AAVE), which can be seen as a form of covert prestige and resistance against dominant sociolinguistic norms. African Americans, when using AAVE, identify themselves as being black through the use of language alone. When used with other African Americans, AAVE can identify the speakers as having shared experiences and some shared aspects of their identities, that is, members of a common in-group. When used with people other than African Americans, AAVE can signal that the listener is not a member of the same in-group. (*AAVE* is usually preferable to *Black English*, as the term *Black English* may lead to the conclusion that all black Americans use the same linguistic variants at all times. Black Americans are usually bi-dialectical, and thus perfectly able to switch from more overtly to covertly prestigious forms of English. The word *vernacular* in AAVE expresses the idea that AAVE is used informally with members of one's in-group.)

When the white American musician Marshall Mathers, better known as Eminem, first gained popularity, much was made of his use of AAVE in his songs. The argument was largely defined by those who saw his use of AAVE as linguistic theft, stealing the lexis, grammar and pronunciation from the African-American speech community. Supporters argued that his AAVE was authentic, and therefore not stealing, because of where he was from, a mostly black neighbourhood in Detroit, rather than because of his skin colour. For his supporters, Mathers' use of AAVE identified him as a working-class resident of his neighbourhood in Detroit, not as an African American.

Reyes (2005) interviewed Asian American young people in a largely black neighbourhood in Philadelphia, some of whom argued that they used AAVE to identify themselves as living similar lives to working-class black Americans, more similar than the lives of middle-class white Philadelphians. As with Mathers, the Asian American interviewees in Reyes' study were clearly not African Americans, yet they used AAVE to **index** themselves as having shared experiences with those whose language they were using. *Index* means "using language to point something out". (People in many cultures, but not all, use their index fingers to point.) One of the youths, Van, told Reyes that she used slang when she was angry and wanted to be "scary", saying that using slang "makes me feel black" (Reyes, 2005, p. 517). Van was pointing out that she used slang to index herself as angry and scary, without having to actually say "I'm angry" explicitly.

People do sometimes index themselves explicitly, such as when they say things like "As a father, I feel..." or "Pensioners find that...", which index the speaker as being either a father or a pensioner, respectively. Ochs (1992) refers to this as **direct indexing**, where the word itself contains a meaning that points to a social variable. The meaning of *father* includes the social variable "male", while *pensioner* includes the social variable "old", in the sense of "old enough to receive a pension". Personal references like *he* and *she* directly index gender, as do titles like *sir*, *miss* and *madame*. Familial terms like *grandmother* and *grandfather* directly index both gender and age.

However, it is not always necessary to be so direct. Language can index speakers or writers as being a certain type of person, in a certain mood, or taking a certain stance without being explicit. Ochs (1992) refers to this as **indirect indexing**. For example, in many English-speaking communities around the world, swearing is associated with masculine language use. This is not to say that women do not swear, but rather that our general association of swearing is that it is something men do. Swearing indirectly indexes the speaker as masculine, even when the speaker is a woman. We would not think that a woman who swears was a man, but we may feel that she is presenting herself as aggressive, for example, a trait commonly associated with men.

For another example, consider how high-pitched voices indirectly index femininity. Some women have lower voices than some men, but on the whole women's voices are higher pitched. A man who wants to sound like a woman will often raise the pitch of his voice, indirectly indexing himself as feminine without actually having to say "I am pretending to be a woman." Interestingly, Ochs (1992, p. 339) cites other research that suggests there is evidence that young girls speak in higher voices than the size of their vocal folds indicates they would do if they spoke without constraint. If this is so, it suggests that even young girls choose to indirectly index themselves as feminine by raising the pitch of their voices.

As Reyes (2005) argues, Van's use of AAVE and slang can only indirectly index herself as being angry and scary by simultaneously indexing African Americans as angry and scary. Without these existing negative stereotypes of African Americans, listeners would have no point of reference to compare with Van's language.

Every time we feel we recognise characteristics of a character in a book or film due to the way his or her language indexes the character, we must be relying on existing linguistic indices between that type of language and that type of person. If the indices are largely positive, it is likely that little offence will be caused. A character who speaks like a scientist will index supposed positive qualities of scientists (intelligence, diligence) and supposed negative ones (social awkwardness). However, relying on overly negative indices, such as when using AAVE to index oneself as angry and scary, and therefore similar to African Americans, is highly contentious. It is not surprising that in cases like this the members of the in-group take offense at use of their language variety by members of an out-group.

Some speech communities go so far as to create an **anti-language**, a covertly prestigious variety that is deliberately designed to exclude members of the out-group. The language of the characters in Anthony Burgess' *A Clockwork Orange* approaches the level of anti-language. The film version of the novel begins with the main character saying the following: "There was me, that is Alex, and my three droogs, that is Pete, Georgie, and Dim, and we sat in the Korova Milkbar trying to make up our rassoodocks what to do with the evening." What are *droogs*, *Milkbars*, and *rassoodocks*? Viewers of the film are immediately confronted with language that separates them linguistically from the speaker. Burgess' characters could not speak too differently from viewers, of course, or audiences would not be able to understand the film. However, Cockney rhyming slang, which provided some inspiration for Burgess' fictional language variety, did often completely exclude those in the out-group.

Exercise – indexing

In the following excerpt from a conversation in a café two friends, young women in their early twenties discuss one's upcoming marriage. How does the language they use index aspects of their social selves?

```
01 C: hey
02 V: hi babe how are you
03 C: oh you look like crap today @
04 V: i'm alright, though i couldn't sleep last night
05 C: gosh i can't believe you're getting married
```

```
07 V: I KNO::W hello i'm mrs leyton <.> where's that husband
08    of mine @ I never see him now that we're married
09 C: out in the shed again @
```

Exercise – indexing (commentary)

The greetings *hey* (line 01) and *hi* (line 02) are informal, which shows us that the speakers are presenting their casual selves to each other. (In different situations we might expect these two to use greetings like "Good morning", "How are you?", and so on. This is discussed in more detail in Chapter 4.) Line 03, although at first instance an insult, is to be taken lightly as it is followed by laughter. V's reaction in line 04 makes no mention of being offended, strengthening this interpretation. V's turn in lines 07 and 08 is of particular interest in terms of how it indexes her. Although she is not yet married, she appears to be saying things that are associated with being married: introducing herself with *mrs* and complaining about her spouse's absence. It makes no sense for her to complain about not seeing her husband when she does not have a husband yet, so the language appears to be simply a means of pointing out that she is soon to be a wife and will soon be saying things wives say. C (line 09) further indexes V as a married woman by imagining that V's husband is to be found working in his shed. (Understanding this depends on knowing that British jokes about absent husbands often play on men's supposed predilection to spend time in their sheds.)

The interpersonal metafunction

In Chapter 2 we saw how the ideational metafunction of language, that is, the ability that language has to communicate meaning, could be described precisely using labels for different processes and participants. However, the metalanguage of *process* and *participant* is not enough to fully describe what happens in any bit of discourse. Consider the following three sentences.

3.1
1. You did read the book.
2. Did you read the book?
3. Read the book.

In all of them the process, *read*, is the same. The participants are also the same, *you* and *the book*. (We understand that *you* is a participant in 3.1.3 although it is not said. This *you* ("You read the book") is an **implied subject**, which is understood to be whomever is being spoken to, perhaps one person, perhaps a group of people being addressed at the same time.) The differences between these clauses is expressed as their grammatical **mood** (Halliday, 2004); they are either declarative, interrogative or imperative.

These three sentences are defined grammatically by the position of the subject and the finite. In the first, 3.1.1, the subject *you* appears before the finite *did*. This is a declarative clause. **The finite** here means "the first word of the verb". It doesn't matter how many words make up the verb, as we only need to see the first word to know that the clause is declarative. In "You should have read the book", the subject *you* and the finite *should* show us that this is a declarative. In "You had been reading the book", the subject *you* and finite *had* show us that this is a declarative. (*Finite* can be a confusing term as it appears similar to related metalinguistic terms like *infinitive* and *finite verb*. For this reason it is usually referred to as *the finite*.)

The finite in declarative clauses is often not visible. When we write "I saw the show", we see only the subject I and the verb saw, but the finite did is understood to be part of the verb saw, which could be realised as the expanded form did see ("I did see the show"). Typically in a declarative clause, we don't say or write the finite, making it visible only when we want to be emphatic. If you said that I didn't meet you at an appointed time, for example at 5 pm, I might reply, "But I did go there at 5 pm", a marked declarative, instead of the less emphatic "But I went there at 5 pm."

Understanding the finite is important when we consider how we recognise other types of clauses. In the second example above, 3.1.2 "Did you read the book?", the subject *you* appears *after* the finite *did*. This is an interrogative clause. In an interrogative clause we typically see one of two possible patterns. First, there is a question word, then the finite, then the subject. "Where did you see her?" = question word *where*, the finite *did*, subject *you*. (Remember, you can identify the subject by rearranging an interrogative clause into a declarative clause. "Where did you see her?" becomes "You did see her where?", putting the subject *you* first in the clause.) "How are they made?" = question word *how*, the finite *are*, subject *they*. "Why was it finished?" = question word *why*, the finite *was*, subject *it*. In the second pattern for interrogative clauses we see the finite followed by the subject, but without any question word. These are yes/no interrogatives. In "Should I stay?" the finite *should* appears before the subject *I*.

The finite provides three pieces of information about the clause that it appears in: the *tense*, the *polarity* and the *modality*. The **tense** is simply whether the clause is past or present. For example, "I meet him for lunch every Thursday" is present tense as the finite is *do*. (*Meet* is *do meet* in its expanded form.) "I met them yesterday" is past tense as the finite is *did*. (*Met* is *did meet* in its expanded form.) The **polarity** is the positive or negative value of the finite: "It was there" is positive while "It wasn't there" is negative. The polarity only concerns the presence or absence of *not* with the finite, it doesn't matter whether the overall meaning of the clause is positive or negative. "Ashia's lost her purse again" displays positive polarity (the finite is *did* as *lost* is expanded to *did lose*), even though it is unfortunate for her that her purse is gone. Similarly, "We didn't expect you to arrive yet" displays negative polarity (the finite is *didn't*), although we may be happy that you've arrived early. The **modality** concerns the presence or absence of modal verbs, which are primarily *may, might, can, could, will, would, shall, should* and *must*. (There are other modal-like expressions such as *ought to* for *should*, *able to* for *can*, and so on, but they mimic the function of the primary modal verbs.) "I am lucky" has no modality (the finite is *am*, which is not a modal verb), while "I should be so lucky" has modality, realised in the modal verb *should*.

To describe the function of modality, it is useful to distinguish between **deontic modality**, which relates to obligation, and **epistemic modality**, which relates to truth. If I say "You should find him before you go home", I am using *should* to suggest something deontic about what you are obliged to do. If I say "You should find him in the pub because he's always there", I am using *should* to suggest something epistemic, that is, "it is probably true that he is in the pub because he is always there". (*Deontic logic* is "the study of obligation, duty and permission", while *epistemology* is "the study of knowledge".)

Returning to example 3.1.3 above ("Read the book"), you will notice that this imperative clause has no subject and no finite. As mentioned, the subject is implied, but can only be understood from the context. (Marked imperatives can feature a subject for emphatic or argumentative purposes (Child A: "Pick it up." Child B: "You pick it up."), but here we are looking at clauses in their usual forms.) We can't say there is a finite in the clause "Read the book" either. We don't understand *when* the book is to be read from the words alone. Perhaps you're being advised to read the book immediately if the speaker is pointing at a book on your table. Perhaps you're being advised to read the book at a convenient time later, if the speaker is trying to convince you that the book version of a story is better than the film version. There is no modality in an imperative as we can't place a modal verb before an imperative. (*"Should read the book" is incorrect.) Imperative clauses do, however, have polarity. ("Read the book" is positive, versus "Don't read the book", which is negative.)

Exercise – mood

Determine the mood of each of the following clauses (declarative, interrogative or imperative) and identify the tense, polarity and modality of the finite in each.

1.   Do you know the way to San Jose?
2.   I've been away so long.
3.   I may go wrong.

Exercise – mood (commentary)

Sentence 1 is interrogative as the finite *do* appears before the subject *you*. The finite *do* displays present tense, positive polarity and no modality. Sentence 2 is declarative as the subject *I* appears before the finite *'ve*. Note that *'ve* is a contraction of *have*, but functions identically. The finite *'ve* displays present tense, positive polarity and no modality. (Don't forget that *have* is present tense. The past tense would be realised as "I had been away so long.") Sentence 3 is declarative as the subject *I* appears before the finite *may*. The finite *may* displays present tense, positive polarity and modality, which here indicates possibility.

Understanding the role of the finite in a clause, and thus whether the clause is declarative, interrogative or imperative, allows us to analyse how the discourse's producer is using grammar to relate the receiver, thus the name interpersonal ("between people") metafunction. In terms of analysing discourse, knowing whether an individual clause is declarative, interrogative or imperative does not tell us much, but looking at clauses in combination does. Consider the following adapted excerpt from Hillary Clinton's speech at the United Nations 4th World Conference on Women.

> Women comprise more than half the world's population. Women are 70 percent of the world's poor, and two-thirds of those who are not taught to read and write. Women are the primary caretakers for most of the world's children and elderly. Yet much of the work we do is not valued – not by economists, not by historians, not by popular culture, not by government leaders.

It is simple enough to say what Ms Clinton was doing here: teaching, lecturing or informing might all be appropriate choices to describe this bit of discourse. However, you should now be able to explain with some precision what defines this as informing. First, these are all declarative clauses. Looking just at the first three clauses, the subject *women* appears before the finites *do* (the verb *comprise* is expanded to *do comprise*), *are*, and *are* in the first three clauses. (Note that there is an elliptical clause *women are* between *and* and *two-thirds* in the second sentence.) These finites all display present tense and positive polarity, making it clear that Ms Clinton is not relaying information about the past, but information that is current. There is no modality in these finites. She is not uncertain about the information; her speech would appear less powerful if she has said "women may comprise", "women might be" and so on. Returning to the ideational metafunction (see Chapter 2), the verbs in these clauses are all relational processes, verbs which serve to connect the subject and the rest of the clause. This is the typical pattern we encounter in informative discourse of this type: declarative mood, little or no modality and many relational processes. (In Chapter 5 we discuss how these clauses' **themes**, the first grammatical element of each clause, also contribute to this discourse. Here each of the first three clauses begins with the same word, *women*.) Most people would, I think, have an intuitive feeling about the nature of this speech, but with the proper linguistic tools we can describe why we know it is so.

Declarative mood is the most commonly realised mood in most discourse, but as we have seen, it is not the only possibility. Some discourses are marked by the appearance of numerous interrogative or imperative clauses. In the following excerpt from Shakespeare's *The Merchant of Venice*, the Jewish character Shylock manipulates grammatical mood in his well-known courtroom speech. "If you prick us do we not bleed? If you tickle us do we not laugh? If you poison us do we not die? And if you wrong us, shall we not revenge?"

These clauses are realised in the interrogative mood. However, readers quickly notice that these are **rhetorical questions**, questions to which the answer is obvious. These are not questions that are asked to be answered, but that are asked to make a point. We know that everyone bleeds when pricked, laughs when tickled and so on. Shylock does not ask these questions expecting a response, but instead to lead his receivers, both the other characters in the play and the audience, to the obvious conclusion that he is their equal.

Similarly, American civil rights campaigner Martin Luther King Jr.'s famous *I Have a Dream* speech features a preponderance of imperative clauses in the following excerpt. "Go back to Mississippi, go back to Alabama, go back to Georgia, go back to Louisiana, go back to the slums and ghettos of our northern cities, knowing that somehow this situation can and will be changed." This is marked by repetition, a rhetorical device that makes the repeated words "go back" memorable, but the repetition in the imperative form makes it clear that this is a prompt for action. Listeners are to return home, taking the message of the speech with them.

Not all texts feature such obviously marked use of a single mood as those we see in the words of Ms Clinton, Shakespeare and Dr King. Typically there will be a variety of moods realised, but we can still use knowledge of mood to define different types of discourse. If you were asked to define a lecture, for example, you might say that someone stands before an audience and talks about a topic. However, you might also explain that a lecture is characterised by certain uses of mood. The lecturer may commonly use declarative mood when discussing the topic ("This is the reason...", "Here are three causes..."), imperative mood to manage the audience ("Look at this example", "Think about the first time...") and interrogative mood to ask questions that he or she plans to answer. In a lecture it is possible to ask the audience to answer questions, but lecturers often pose questions, allow the audience a brief moment to think, then provide an answer for the audience to consider. In a job interview, we might expect to see interrogative mood used by the interviewers ("What qualifications do you have?") while the applicant responds with declarative mood ("I worked for three years at..."). A narrative would typically feature declarative mood to explain a linked sequence of events ("Goldilocks entered the cottage", "She saw three bowls", "Then she ate the porridge.").

If you went to purchase a recipe book, you'd have certain expectations about the grammatical mood you'd encounter in the book. Looking back to the recipe in Chapter 1, you'll see it is characterised by imperative mood: "*heat* the sunflower oil", "*use* a larger pan", "*fry* the garlic" and so on. Imperative mood is a characteristic feature of this genre of text. The same words realised in a different mood would seem unusual in that book. The use of the declarative mood ("The chef heats the oil") might seem more rightly to be a story about cooking. The use of the interrogative mood ("Will you heat the oil?") might be characteristic of two people cooking together. We don't only know a recipe book is a recipe book because it says so on its cover. We need to be convinced by the language used within it. Grammatical mood is one linguistic element that helps convince us.

Stance

When we use language, we can be firm, be tentative, suggest things, argue points, accept or reject another's argument and so on. In linguistic terms, we take a **stance** when we use language.

According to Strauss and Feiz (2014, p. 275), "stance is the speaker's or writer's feeling, attitude, perspective, or position as enacted in the discourse". The concepts discussed in the previous section of this chapter (subject, finite and grammatical mood) allow us to describe stance with some precision. Any subject and finite combination tells us how the producer is relating to the audience. When two young children argue, they produce things like the following.

3.2
```
01 L: you broke it
02 M: did not
03 L: did too
04 M: didn't
05 L: you must've you had it last
```

In line 01, *L* accuses a subject "you" using "broke", which includes the finite *did* (broke = did break). The finite *did* tells us the tense (past), polarity (positive) and modality. In this case there is no modality, making *L* seem certain about this. The finite "did" in line 01 sets the parameters of the exchange. *M* could argue about the tense ("You break everything") or the modality ("I might have broken it"), but in this case, *M* chooses to argue about the polarity, changing "did" into "did not". Both speakers reaffirm their stances in lines 03 and 04, committing themselves to a discussion of whether or not the polarity is positive or negative. In line 05, *L* introduces modality into the exchange with the new finite "must". (Here "must" expresses a deduction or logical connection, that is, something similar to "You had it last, so I deduce that you broke it.")

Using a modal verb such as *must* in the finite position is one way of modifying one's stance. Butt *et al.* (2000) list two more common modifications: mood adjuncts (p. 115) and interpersonal grammatical metaphors (p. 116). The first, mood adjuncts, are relatively simple to explain. *Adjunct* means "extra" or "supplemental", so **mood adjuncts** are extra, grammatically unnecessary words that modify the mood. Consider the difference between "He always smokes outside the office", "He sometimes smokes outside the office" and "He never smokes outside the office." The subject *he* and the finite *does* (*smokes* = *does* + *smoke*) have not changed here. However, the mood adjuncts *always*, *sometimes* and *never* tell us more about how usual it is for him to be smoking.

Here are some common purposes of mood adjuncts, along with some words, usually adverbs, that fulfil those purposes.

usual = always, often, sometimes, rarely, never
probable = probably, likely, possibly, unlikely
obvious = obviously, of course, surely, indeed

If you are invited to a friend's birthday party and you respond with "Of course I'll go", you've indicated how obvious your affirmative response is with the mood adjunct *of course*. You could have just said "I'll go", which would also indicate an affirmative response, but the addition of *of course* to your subject *I* and finite *will* makes your stance, in this case your positive feeling about the event, clearly visible in the discourse.

Another common way of modifying stance is to use an interpersonal grammatical metaphor. Despite the complexity of the name, this is neither an unusual stance modification nor is it difficult to understand, for the most part. The song title *I Think We're Alone Now*, first sung by Tommy James and the Shondells, exemplifies this modification of stance. The "I think" clause in the title is not really a comment on the singer's thinking process. Instead it means "probably", so we interpret the title as meaning "We're probably alone now." Compare that *think* to *think* in "It's so noisy I can't think", in which *think* refers to the brain's capacity for cognitive function. They are clearly different uses of *think*. So an **interpersonal grammatical metaphor** sees the use of an entire grammatical clause ("I think") in a metaphorical, non-literal sense (*think* means "probably", not "using the brain") to modify the producer's interpersonal stance towards the receiver. (In the "Cognitive discourse markers" section of Chapter 5, *I think* is discussed again, in particular the difference between "I think..." and "I think...".)

You understand the interpersonal grammatical metaphor concept if you can distinguish between the function of *believe* in the following two sentences, both taken from A.A. Milne's *Winnie the Pooh*.

3.3
1. "Was that me?" said Christopher Robin in an awed voice, hardly daring to believe it.
2. When Eeyore saw the pot, he became quite excited. "Why!" he said. "I believe my balloon will just go into that pot!"

In 3.3.1 *believe* means "accept that something is true". This is the denotational meaning of belief. In 3.3.2 *believe* in the clause "I believe" is used as a metaphor for "likely", so we interpret Eeyore's final clause as "My balloon will likely just go into that pot." This use of *believe* expresses Eeyore's uncertain stance; he's not sure if the balloon will fit or not.

Chapter 4

Thinking about the Context

In this chapter we look at *register*, which is the description of how language varies according to the situation in which it is used. We do not always speak or write the same way, but take account of who our receivers are and the purpose of the language event. We also look at how discourses with similar purposes and similar features can be described in terms of their *genre*.

My name is *Sean*, but when I was young my parents would sometimes call me by my full name, *William Sean Sutherland*. Whenever they did so, I would immediately have the feeling that something was wrong. Both *Sean* and *William Sean Sutherland* are acceptable vocatives to call me, but hearing my full name would tell me something about the context that the word was used in. My full name meant I was in trouble, while *Sean* alone didn't convey that. Even now, I rarely hear my full name. I encounter it in its written form on official documents like my passport and in letters from my bank, but I can't recall hearing it since I got married a decade ago. ("Do you, William Sean Sutherland, agree...") My full name is often indicative of formal situations where it is important to identify me precisely. There are many *Seans*, some *Sean Sutherlands*, but few *William Sean Sutherlands*. When my parents wanted to make it perfectly clear that I, and no other *Sean*, was in trouble, they'd use my full name. This association is now very strong in my understanding of my name. If a police officer appeared at my door and asked for me by my full name, I would likely start to worry.

I'm also sometimes known by the informal diminutive, *Seannie*. This makes my name longer by three letters, but it can be called a **diminutive** because the purpose of *Seannie* is to make me *seem* smaller, unthreatening and more endearing. We use diminutives like this with children's names (*Johnnie, Vicky*), with things for children (*bikkie, rubber ducky*) and with animals that we want to identify as small and cuddly (*doggie, kitty*). As you can guess, I'm only known as *Seannie* to a small group of people. My wife calls me *Seannie*, but no one in my office does. However, my daughter picked up on this form of my name from my wife, my nieces at the same school learned it from my daughter, and now half of the children in the school seem to call me that. Inevitably when they do call me *Seannie* their parents will correct them, saying to call me *Mr Sutherland* or at least *Sean*.

What these children's parents are doing is teaching them about **register**, which is language variation based on use (Halliday, 1978). There is no universally correct name for me. In casual use I'm *Sean*. More formally I'm *Sean Sutherland*. Most formally I'm *Mr William Sean Sutherland*. Sometimes at work I'm *Dr Sutherland*. The right name for me depends on the context in which someone wants to name me. When children call me *Seannie*, it sounds funny (and cheeky children often do so knowing it is funny) because the register is inappropriate. Children don't normally use diminutives for adults. When people with PhDs use the title *Dr* outside of their work, when booking a hotel room, for example, they may be mocked for pretentiousness because the title *Dr* has no relevance to the context of choosing a room. The right language should be used for the right context or it sounds wrong: funny, pretentious or whatever else the case may be.

The analysis of register is not only concerned with names. Grammar, word choice and phonology are all part of our determination of how one register might differ from another. The following three sentences all communicate roughly the same information, but they do so in different ways.

1. "I've got your note. Thanks."
2. "Thank you. I have received your message."
3. "Your letter has been received."

Sentence 1 uses a contraction (*I've*) while the others don't. Using contractions is generally seen as less formal than not using them. (You may have noticed that in this book contractions are used for the most part, which may contribute to a general feeling that the book is somewhat chatty and informal.) The word *note* is used in sentence 1, while in sentence 2 *message* is used. These words may not be perfectly synonymous (a *note* is written, while a *message* could be spoken or written), but here their senses seem the same. However, *note* is a one-syllable word while *message* is two syllables. We tend to treat longer words as being more formal than shorter ones, although this is not always the case. Here the more consistent use of shorter words (*got, note, thanks*) in sentence 1 is markedly different than the longer forms in sentence 2 (*received, message, thank you*).

Both sentence 1 and sentence 2 are realised in the active voice, while sentence 3 is realised in the passive voice. The active voice is more common in many genres of text, but the passive voice is common in more formal, impersonal discourse, such as academic writing, lab reports and letters from banks and other businesses. In sentence 3 it is not clear who received the message.

No individual linguistic feature should be taken as indicative of a certain register. Rather, the overall combination of features helps us make a final determination. Sentence 1 feels like an informal comment or email, sentence 2 feels more formal, yet still personal. Both 1 and 2 are examples of **phatic communication**, meaning language used for social purposes. The producer is using language here to be polite. Sentence 3 is an example of **institutional language**, meaning language, used by the members of an organisation, that shows they are speaking or writing on behalf of their institution (business, hospital, university, etc.), not as individuals.

Note – active voice and passive voice

Active voice and passive voice differ in the placement of the subject and the **agent** (the thing that is doing something) in a clause. In the active voice sentence "I ate the apple", the personal reference *I* is both the subject, as it appears before the verb *ate* in this declarative clause, and the agent, as *I* is the thing that did the eating. (More precisely, we could say that *I* appears before the finite *did*, as *ate* is *did eat* in its expanded form.)

In the passive voice sentence "The apple was eaten by me", the subject is *the apple*, for this is the noun phrase that appears before the verb *was eaten*. However, we understand that the apple did not do anything here. Here, *the apple* is **the patient**, the person or the thing to which something was done. The action of eating was done to the apple *by me*, so *by me* is the agent. In the active voice the subject and agent are the same, while in the passive voice the subject and the agent are different. Some passive voice clauses don't have an agent. In "The apple was eaten", the subject is *the apple*, but there is no agent as we don't know who did the eating, hence the name **agentless passive**.

Style guides, that is, books that advise writers on how to write, often suggest avoiding the passive voice. The active voice is said to be more dynamic and it is sometimes more accurate, but there is a place for the passive voice. When we don't know who or what did something, we use the passive voice, as in "My bike's been stolen." (*My bike* is the subject, but we don't know which agent stole it.) The passive voice is also useful when we want to emphasise the patient, as in "The three children were taken to the hospital." (*The three children* are the patient here as the taking was done to them; the agent was perhaps their parents or the ambulance, but the writer has decided that this is not necessary information.) Most famously, the passive voice is used for obfuscation. American president Richard Nixon famously used the words "Mistakes were made" when discussing political shenanigans within his administration, which admitted the existence of mistakes, but said nothing about who made them.

Register

While it is clear that people use language differently at different times, and thus use different registers, it is not always as clear how to define register. Trudgill (1983, p. 101) wrote that variation related to "occupations, professions or topics have been termed registers". This definition is a good starting point, for it is often clear that people's work affects the language they use, especially when they are at work. When someone argues about small details, they might be accused of speaking like a lawyer, while someone long-winded and didactic might be called "Professor" to tease them. This shows that we have certain preconceptions about how members of certain professions speak.

In common parlance we might talk about someone having a *heart attack*, while doctors, nurses and other medics commonly use *myocardial infarction*. The medical register is more precise here, for it gives those who know more information: *myo* means "muscle", *cardial* means "heart" and *infarction* means "blocked blood flow". Serious cases might be referred to as *acute myocardial infarction*, which provides yet more precise information to a medical specialist. Specialist language like this is sometimes dismissively referred to as **jargon**, overly complex language designed to make the user seem more intelligent. (To borrow Shakespeare's words, jargon is language that is "full of sound and fury, signifying nothing".) In reality, language specific to certain occupations often gives its users more precise information. As I wrote earlier, when speaking to children or other non-specialists I sometimes say that *phonology* is "the study of the sounds of English". However, a cough is a sound, a knock on the door is a sound, and a laugh is a sound, but none of these is phonologically meaningful.

It is important to point out that no register is objectively any better than any other register. Register is often described as "the right language for the right situation", where *situation* means the same thing as "context". If a doctor tells someone that his or her mother has suffered *an acute myocardial infarction*, without explaining that this means "heart attack", it may be felt that the doctor is being unnecessarily complex, and thus using language to belittle or exclude. It might be more appropriate when speaking with a patient to say *heart attack*, saving the medical register for use with other medical professionals.

A particular register may in fact be designed to exclude others, as in the case related to me by a worker on the London Underground, who explained that the announcement "There's one under on the hot and cold at GPS" meant "There is a person under the train on the Hammersmith and City Line at Great Portland Street station." Here the lexical choices were made to inform workers about the situation while avoiding causing alarm to passengers.

In the case of ordering coffee at Starbucks, which was mentioned briefly in Chapter 1, the coffee chains' employees and customers may have different feelings about the appropriate register. Customers who order a "small coffee" may find that an employee recasts the order as a "tall coffee". (**Recast** means "to correct someone's language use by rephrasing it in a different way". It's what language teachers do when a student says "I goed" and the teacher replies with "You went.") Customers may resist using "tall" to describe a smaller-sized coffee, which shows us that "the right language" is a subjective concept, although it may be based on widely held views.

Trudgill's (1983) definition of register also mentioned "topics" as being particularly pertinent to register. There may be subtle or gross shifts in language use depending on what is being discussed or written about. In English there is the interesting distinction made between words for food and words for animals from which the food originates. We talk about *cows* and *sheep* when they are animals in a field, but *beef* and *mutton* (or *lamb*) when we are going to eat those same animals. Asking someone "Do you want to eat pig?" would seem register-inappropriate, and thus an indication of either poor language skills or as an attempt at humour.

This division in register between animals in the field and food on the plate tells us something about the linguistic history of the English language. English is a language of Germanic origin with a layer of French–Latin vocabulary added later. *Cow* is Germanic (German "kuh") while *beef* is Latin (French "beouf"). When the Norman French conquered England, their words began to displace Germanic-origin words in some situations. Imagine an English peasant trying to sell cows to a French knight or lord. The word *cow* might not be understood, but using the word *beouf*, mispronounced as "beef," could lead to communication and a sale.

French-derived words tend to be used in formal situations, situations calling for more precision, and situations that call for linguistic cleanliness. Asking someone to eat *pork* (French "porc"), with the connotations of taste and sophistication that are associated with French food, is more polite than *pig*, with its connotations of mud and dirt. (When we want to be particularly sophisticated, we revert to using the actual French words, such as *beouf bourguignon* for the dish and other French words in restaurant names.)

The French–German division is not only visible in words for food. A *teacher* (Germanic) and a *professor* (French) are the same in many ways, but *teachers* are associated with primary and secondary school, while *professors* are associated with "higher" learning. (To be clear, I'm not saying that professors are better than teachers in any way, only that the words have certain connotations based on current linguistic use and history.) As a general rule, the Germanic words tend to be shorter, high-frequency words, such as *buy*. The Latin–French words such as *purchase* tend to be longer, low-frequency words. **High-frequency** means "used often" while **low-frequency** means "used rarely." A corpus linguistics researcher might provide some accurate data about how often *buy* is used in comparison to *purchase*. For a rough estimation, a Google search turns up twice as many hits for *buy* as for *purchase*.

Another way of looking at register is to consider what Joos (1967) called the five "styles" of English. Instead of focusing on professions and topics, as Trudgill's definition does, Joos looked more broadly at how pronunciation, vocabulary, grammar, evidence of planning or spontaneity, the language structure and the type of information all contribute to our interpretation of different discourses as belonging to different registers. Joos' five categories are problematic in some ways. As with many categorical answers, the determination that there were five categories may have been chosen for convenience more than for total accuracy. (If we divide language use into too few categories, such as simply *formal* or *informal*, we can't provide enough detail about variation. If we divide language into too many categories, such as eight, nine or more, we may find that it is difficult to remember them. Many linguistic concepts are divided into three, four or five simply because it is a useful number of categories to remember and work with.) In addition, Joos did not always provide evidence to back up his claims about language use. Nevertheless, if we want to know the historical development of the concept of variation according to use, it is important to be familiar with Joos' five styles.

Frozen – This is language which does not change. Words are often archaic, unused outside of special circumstances, and grammar may be marked. The traditional wedding vow from the Christian *Book of Common Prayer* begins with "With this ring, I thee wed." *Thee* is an archaic marked variant of the pronoun *you* in its object form. The word itself is marked (we rarely hear *thee* outside of a church), as is its placement before the verb *wed*, which is also marked. A modern translation would be "I marry you." Folk songs are also often frozen. The children's rhyme that contains "Pease porridge hot, pease porridge cold" is similarly frozen. Other than when reciting the rhyme, few people use the word *pease*, preferring the more modern *pea* and *peas*.

Note – count and non-count nouns

Pease is a **non-count noun**, also known as a **mass noun**, used for things that we don't usually count, such as *milk* or *furniture*. We say "We need some new furniture", not "We need two new furniture." We can of course say "two bottles of milk", but now we are counting *bottles*, not the milk itself. *Pea* and *peas* are **count nouns**, which as the name implies can be counted. (It is probably that the mass noun *pease* came to be thought of as being the plural *peas*, which later led to the singular *pea*.) The plural form of count nouns can take a number as a modifier ("one chair, two chairs", etc.) while non-count nouns can't ("some furniture", not *"two furniture").

Formal – This is the language of official situations. It is usually considered "one-way", in that the producer is the only one participating in the language event, so published written works are formal, but planned spoken discourse is also often formal. Ellipsis (Chapter 1), implicature (Chapter 5) and other potential areas of ambiguity are avoided, since the receivers may not be able to ask questions, either because they are not present if they are reading or because they are not expected to do so, as in a formal speech. The first sentence of JRR Tolkien's *The Lord of the Rings* begins like this: "When Mr. Bilbo Baggins of Bag End announced that he would shortly be celebrating his eleventy-first birthday with a party of special magnificence, there was much talk and excitement in Hobbiton." This formal language use is largely characterised by what we don't see: there are no grammatical errors, there are no contractions (we see "he would", not "he'd") and there is no response from the reader. In addition, the sentence is quite long and contains several clauses, which are centred on the verbs *announced, would be celebrating* and *was*. It is difficult to produce language like this without some planning. Producers of formal discourse often avoid relying on what Cutting (2002) called interpersonal and cultural context (see Chapter 2) as they may not know their receivers, and thus can't be sure of what information they share with them. They may also avoid referring to the situational context (Cutting, 2002) as they are often not in the same place as those receivers, especially in the case of a written text.

Consultative – The register used in polite conversation with strangers, with acquaintances and even with friends in somewhat formal situations. The discourse is two-way: spoken interactions such as shopping or dealing with colleagues and written interactions such as exchanging emails with business contacts or institutions. As the discourse involves more than one producer we would expect to see the use of cohesive devices to connect turns. Here we may see evidence of spontaneity in the discourse, so grammatical errors, mispronunciations and imprecise word choices may appear, but speakers may repair errors they've made, taking care to speak or write properly. The long, grammatically complex sentences that appear in the formal register are less common as there is less time for careful planning. Shared cultural context may be evident as we know who we are communicating with (a clerk in a shop, the customer service representative of an institution), but shared interpersonal context is less likely to be as we may not know much about that person as an individual. The topic is often specific as the speakers or writers have an **instrumental purpose**, meaning they want to accomplish something concrete with their interaction.

Casual – The language used with friends and close acquaintances. Word choice may be very general ("guys", "stuff", etc.) and anaphoric reference to previous conversations is possible ("How was that thing you told me about?"), as the speakers rely on mutual shared interpersonal knowledge and thus don't need to be as explicit as when speaking with strangers. Slang words and swearing may appear in the lexis, both things which are usually avoided with strangers or in polite situations. Function words, especially at the beginning of turns, may be omitted ("Wanna eat now?" instead of the consultative "Do you want to eat now?"). Polite language features, such as the use of *please*, can be omitted without causing offense. Contractions, although possible in other registers, become common; using full forms such as *cannot* and *do not* may seem purposefully unfriendly. The android named Data, a character in the *Star Trek* series of science-fiction television programmes, speaks English fluently, although he (it?) can't use contractions. This was meant to characterise the character as emotionless and cold. (Children seem to instinctively associate contractions with warmth and humanity. They almost always say, "I am a robot" when they are play-acting, not "I'm a robot.") Topics may include gossip and other social talk, and topics may change rapidly, as the primary purpose of the inter-action is phatic rather than instrumental.

Note – slang

The linguistic distinction between *informal* words and *slang* is usually made in terms of the stability of the words and the numbers of people who use and understand them. Informal words change meaning only slowly, as with formal words. In addition, informal words are known to everyone, although they may only be used in certain registers. Slang, on the other hand, changes rapidly, with new meanings replacing older ones and with some terms disappearing from use entirely. Slang words are known and used by specific speech communities, with other people either not knowing them at all or only being somewhat familiar through hearsay.

Some slang words eventually see their meanings stabilise and become known to all, thus becoming informal. New terms for money, a very productive source of slang, such as the British word *quid* ("one pound Sterling") and American *buck* ("one dollar", also used in other countries), are now stable and widely known, so don't feel like slang anymore. On the other hand, the slang term *money*, meaning "excellent", seems to have peaked in use in the 1990s, then dis-appeared. (See the 1996 film *Swingers* for evidence of this word being popular at that time.)

Intimate – This is the private language used by spouses, lovers, par-ents with children, and others who share long-term positive social bonds. This is heavily dependent on interpersonal knowledge, but otherwise shares many characteristics of casual language use. However, the use of slang tends to decrease with social intimates. We don't always need to use language to index ourselves as belong-ing to a certain group, one of the main purposes of slang, with those to whom we are so clearly socially connected. In excerpt 4.1, we see several references to shared knowledge (What is "it" (line 01)? , who is "he" (line 02) and "how" is he (line 02)?, what time is "back early" (line 03)), as well as idiosyncratic family-specific lexis ("do huggies" (line 03)).

4.1

```
01 husband: How was it?
02 wife:    Fine. You know how he is.
03 child:   Mama's back early. Good. Time to do huggies.
```

Register as field, tenor and mode

Joos' five styles of language, which I have repurposed here as five registers, is sometimes criticised for being too strictly categorical, meaning that this conception of register attempts to divide language use precisely into one of the five styles when it is not always possible to say with clarity which is the most accurate label for a certain instance of language use. Joos' registers force us to divide language into discrete, separate categories, when it may be better to think of language use as existing on a continuum of possibilities. A text message exchange, for example, may exhibit some features of casual language and some of intimate language, making it impossible to decide which is the better label.

A final system for discussing register, one which takes more account of the difficulty of placing a language event clearly in one category, is the division of register into field, tenor and mode. Butt *et al.* (2000, p. 5) describe these three elements of register as follows: field is "what is to be talked or written about"; tenor is "the relationship between the speaker and the hearer"; and mode is "the kind of text that is being made". As they argue, a change to any one of these will lead to changes in the text.

The **field** is the topic of the language event. This can be interpreted quite narrowly, so *a hammer*, *a Christmas carol* or *a burglary* are all examples of *field*. We can also think of *field* as a broader term, covering a wider range of experiences. So a product catalogue of tools, including hammers, might be conceptualised as belonging to the field of *construction*, singing a Christmas carol could be seen as belonging to the field of *religious celebration*, and a witness' discussion of a burglary might be more broadly named as belonging to the field of *police work*.

It is important to note that there is no master list of fields to which all language events must belong. Analysts look at the words in the discourse and make judgements about which semantic field or fields they belong to, then assign a label that most accurately represents that field. Should a church choir singing a Christmas carol be thought of as belonging to the field of *religious celebration*, *Christian religious life* or simply *religion*, for example? Certain words (*worship*, *holy*) may indicate religion, others (*joy*, *rejoice*) may indicate celebration, while yet more (*Jesus*, *Bethlehem*) may be indicative of Christianity. The description has to balance being precise with being general enough to show that this particular event shares features with other similar language events.

We can also consider whether the words used to discuss the topic are words of a general nature, high-frequency lexis known to all, or are specific, low-frequency words that indicate the text is part of specialist discourse. Hughes (1990) provides examples of general words with their more specialist equivalents: *crime* and *larceny* (larceny means "taking someone's property"), *hole* and *orifice* (*orifice* is "an opening in a body") and *speed* and *velocity* (*velocity* means "the measurement of speed and direction"). We shouldn't consider only one word when trying to decide whether the discourse is general or specific; we must consider the whole text. Hearing words like *speed*, *turn* and *weight* might be characteristic of a fan's general discussion of the field of car racing, while the roughly comparable words *velocity*, *angle* and *mass* might be more likely in an automotive engineering course.

The film *Monty Python and the Holy Grail* derived some of its humour from manipulating our expectations of field-specific language. The following excerpt, from a fictional Biblical *Book of Armaments* referenced in the film, contains words from several semantic fields that we would not normally expect to see together: "Saint Attila raised the hand grenade up on high, saying, 'O Lord, bless this thy hand grenade, that with it thou mayst blow thine enemies to tiny bits, in thy mercy.' And the Lord did grin." Hand grenades are anachronistic to the Bible's time, while "blow... to tiny bits" and "grin" don't seem like Biblical language. "Tiny" and "grin" don't appear in the *New International Version*, while "bits" appears only twice, once meaning "the tool that is used to guide a horse", not "small piece". Words with similar meanings do appear (*small*, *smile* and *pieces*), so it is clear that those concepts appear in the Christian Bible, but some words are not used in that register.

The **tenor** element of the register is the social relationship between the producer(s) and the receiver(s) of the discourse. In short, the way we write and speak changes when readers and listeners change, even when the field has not changed. Discussions of tenor are primarily concerned with how formal or informal the discourse is. (In fact, *register* is sometimes taken to mean "formality level". If we are too formal or too informal, others may think something is wrong, which leads to the idea that formality is the most salient aspect of register.) When you choose to address someone as *Sir, Madam, Mr, Mrs, Doctor*, or by a given name, surname, nickname and so on, you're considering the tenor of the discourse. You make the choice based on how well you know the person and on the context in which you find yourself writing or speaking. Normally I initiate an email exchange with people I don't know by referring to them as *Mr* or *Ms So-and-so*. Later, as our relationship develops to one of acquaintance, I may begin to use their given names. However, if I talk about that person with someone else I may revert to the more formal *Mr* or *Mrs* again, to avoid seeming disrespectful when talking about someone who is not present.

Formality is about more than just the vocative used. Colloquial words are usually considered informal. A doctor acknowledges the formality of the context when discussing an adult patient's health problems by using words like *defecate* and *urinate* instead of *pee* and *poo*. The formal words indicate the social distance between the doctor and the patient; we normally only use *pee* and *poo* with children or people we know well. With people we don't know well or don't know at all, we may avoid mentioning this taboo topic, preferring **euphemisms** like "Where's the rest room?", which avoids mentioning waste elimination entirely. Of course, a doctor may use *pee* and *poo* when talking to an unhealthy child. The doctor must consider the field of the discourse, the child's presumed knowledge of specialist language in that field, and then make choices about tenor accordingly. (Field, tenor and mode must all be accounted for at the same time. Although they are separate elements of register, they are interrelated; changes to one element can affect the others.)

Other linguistic features that are generally considered **markers of informality** are contractions and abbreviations, vague words like *a lot* (formally it would be best to give a precise number or at least an estimate), spoken discourse markers (see Chapter 5) like *well* and *you know* (especially in written language), phrasal verbs (*look at* and *back up* are less formal than *examine* and *reverse*) and the use of *I* ("I believe..." is less formal than "It is believed..."). Some punctuation is considered informal, primarily exclamations marks and the use of long dashes in place of commas. Grammatical patterns can be judged in terms of formality, too. The active voice is common in all registers, but passive voice usually marks formal writing, especially in academic writing. None of these should be considered inherently less formal than their more formal variants. Longer, low-frequency Latin-based words are not naturally more formal than shorter, high-frequency Germanic words. It is the historical development of the language that led to this current understanding of their formality.

Misjudging the tenor of the relationship can lead to a register that may annoy receivers or create distance between them and the producer. A certain amount of formality is expected in a job interview; the candidate who is too informal won't be hired. A funeral service does not have to be entirely formal, but too much informality will seem disrespectful to the dead. Thornbury (2005) provides the example of an epitaph on a churchyard gravestone which the church vicar judged to be too informal as it included the words *dad* and *granddad* instead of *father* and *grandfather*. A judge ruled in the vicar's favour, so this was not just an idiosyncratic individual.

When students write emails to me and don't use any form of address or sign off with their own names, I can become irritated. I don't expect them to write *Dear Dr. Sutherland* and *Yours sincerely, Chloe,* or whatever the name might be, with every email (I'm not so vain or pompous, I think), but a simple *Hi Sean* at the beginning of the message acknowledges that we have a relationship, while not including a greeting feels very impersonal. A generic sign on a wall does not address you by name as it does not have a personal relationship with you. Otherwise, some personalisation is reasonable. When judging the correct tenor we must not only consider what we feel the relationship to be, but we must also project ourselves into the receiver's self and consider the relationship from his or her point of view.

Some students do email me or talk to me and do call me *sir* or *Dr. Sutherland*, even when I tell them that it is not necessary to be so formal. (My students are not children, but young adults aged 18 years and above.) I think they are imagining the interaction from my point of view and deciding that the more formal forms of address are something I would appreciate, even when I say they are not necessary. Fairclough (1989) makes a distinction between the power *in* the discourse and the power *behind* the discourse, which may help explain this. In class I have the most power, which is reflected in the discourse: I control the content of the class by deciding what to talk about ("Today I would like to cover three important topics...") and I manage the classroom behaviour with language ("Who can answer this?", "Please look at section four", and so on). However, even without reading or hearing what I say, people know that teachers are in charge of their classrooms, that is, they recognise the power behind the discourse. I may tell students in the discourse that they need not call me *sir*, but their awareness of my power behind the discourse (I control their grades) leads them to use the formal address even when I ask them not to.

When discussing tenor, it is also productive to look at whether the producer addresses the receiver as an equal or from a position of authority. We don't tend to want to sound bossy or pushy when we talk to those whom we see as our equals or superiors, so we may **hedge,** that is, use linguistic devices that reduce the force of what we say. An employee talking to his or her manager can make suggestions sound less authoritative in a variety of ways (the hedges in the following are in italics): by starting with hedging clauses ("*I think* the decision to buy is...", "*It appears that* the best choice is..."), using modal verbs ("It *may* be best...", "We *could* consider buying..."), and modifying with adverbs ("probably") and adjectives ("possible"). On the other hand, such linguistic devices would sound odd if used too often by one who was expected to be an authority. Would you trust a teacher who said "Two plus two is *likely* four" and "The Earth *might* revolve around the Sun?"

https://eflfunc.wordpress.com/2013/04/10/tenor-of-discourse/

A language user will sometimes pretend to be an equal with his audience before revealing his authority. Consider once again the words *speed* and *velocity*, which may be used interchangeably by non-specialists. Those with expertise in the maths and sciences will recognise that *speed* only measures how quickly something moves, while *velocity* measures speed and the displacement from the starting point. (Children who run across a field and back have a measurable speed as they run, but their final velocity is zero as they have returned to their starting points.) A teacher who wishes to explain the concept of *velocity* to children may judge their schematic knowledge (see Chapter 2) to be insufficient, and so may start by discussing *speed* or using common words like *fast* and *slow* before introducing the new concept, *velocity*.

I have focused so far mostly on spoken discourse, but all discourses contain an element of tenor, including written ones such as signs. Signs on waste disposal receptacles in Britain may say "deposit rubbish here", with *rubbish* being an acknowledgement of an interaction with an expected British audience, while American signs may say "trash only", using the American English variant *trash*. The text on the sign is part of a discourse that includes the context, which in this case is the country, and the variant used signals this relationship between the producer of the sign and the its receivers. Signs in the southern parts of the United States sometimes say "trash only / basura solamente", an acknowledgement that the relationship that exists includes readers who may read English or Spanish.

The final element of register in this approach is the **mode**, which is the type of text being made. At the most general level the mode is either written or spoken for most people. (The gestural mode, most often sign language but also including referee's signals in sports, police and military hand signals, and related forms of communication made with the hands, arms, face and body, is a third mode of communication.) We can further divide each of the two mains modes into narrower divisions. The written mode includes poetry and prose, prose includes newspapers and books, books include fiction and non-fiction, non-fiction includes biographies and recipe books and so on. The spoken mode includes conversations, speeches, debates, sales calls, concerts, comedy shows and plays.

In reality, some forms of discourse can't clearly be said to be either entirely written or spoken. A politician's speech, religious leader's sermon or business person's sales pitch is often written first, but delivered in the spoken mode. Sometimes when a politician speaks, he or she will read a speech, but also deviate from it, perhaps making errors while doing so. Journalists and public relations officers may then argue over which mode was the official one: the written one that was meant to be read or the spoken one that was actually produced. Back-and-forth email exchanges, while obviously written, exhibit many features of the spoken mode. Tellingly, email programmes and general usage confirm that we see email exchanges as being at least partly spoken, for it is common to refer to these exchanges as "conversations" and to say that we were "talking" to someone by email. Text messages are even more "conversation-like" in mode.

To overcome this conflation of speech and writing in some modes, it is productive to discuss the discourse in terms of how spontaneous or planned it is. **Spontaneous** discourse, as the name suggests, is produced quickly and without much forethought. The focus is on the content of the discourse, sometimes at the expense of linguistic accuracy. When we engage in friendly conversation, we tend to speak quickly, sometimes up to three words per second, and don't always concentrate on producing language that is grammatically accurate and lexically precise. People say things like "There is three reasons" instead of "There are three reasons", use general nouns like *stuff* and *things* instead of more precise words, and favour verbs with broad meanings like *have*, *do* and *get*. (Consider *have lunch* ("eat"), *have a cold* ("be afflicted with"), *have a car* ("possess") and *have a child* ("be the parent of"). In quick speech, we may prefer to use *have* and rely on our listener(s) interpreting which sense is correct, rather than spending time choosing the word with the narrowest, most precise meaning.) While these features of spontaneous language are common in speech, some written modes are also produced spontaneously, with a focus on content over form. A colleague sent me an email that read "hello Sean. If you're got time I'm sure it would be better on this Friday." I'm sure she knows that normally *hello* would be capitalised, *you're* should be *you've*, and that only *on* or *this* was needed, but she wanted to communicate something quickly and was not concerned about these errors of form that don't interfere with the content of her message. It is true that these are errors, but I know from previous experience that she, a trained linguist, could write with complete accuracy if she wanted to. We often agree implicitly in this mode to ignore such linguistic lapses. People will have different ideas about how spontaneous emails, text messages, social networking status updates, etc., should be, so the tenor element of the register must also be considered when we think about spontaneity. I'm less tolerant of errors in emails that students send me, for example, as I'm responsible for monitoring and trying to improve their language use in a way that I'm not responsible for my colleagues.

Planned discourse, on the other hand, is often marked by what is missing: few or no grammatical errors, fewer words with broad meanings, and little evidence of language repair. (Mistakes in written discourse are erased and re-written, unlike in spoken discourse when we must say "What I mean is..." and so on if we wish to rephrase something.) Longer, grammatically complex sentences with several clauses are common. The language we see or hear will tend to adhere more closely to our notions of standard English. Written discourses tend to be more planned than spoken ones, but some spoken ones such as graduation speeches, public announcements on train and airplane services, and class lectures are all often planned. As with spontaneous discourse, we have certain expectations of the "correct" register in these situations. Students who hear a lecture that is too spontaneous (the *mode* element of the register) may be disappointed, feeling that the professor has not planned for what is a serious topic (the *field* element of the register) in a more formal context (the *tenor* element of register). Airline flight attendants who exhibit more spontaneous discourse when they make pre-flight safety announcements are often appreciated by passengers; a normally planned and repetitive language event is enlivened and personalised.

Note – author, writer, audience and reader

Hoey (2001) provides us with the useful distinction that can be made between *author* and *writer* and between *audience* and *reader*. The first distinction, between author and writer, concerns the producer(s) of the text. The **author** is the authority behind the production of the text, that is, the one who chooses the content and takes responsibility for it. The **writer** is the person (or people) who produces the words of the text. The author and the writer are sometimes the same, as in the case of most novels. Charles Dickens came up with the ideas in his novels and wrote the words to represent those ideas. Sometimes, the author and writer are not the same. A politician may be the author of a policy speech in that he or she speaks the words and puts the support of his or her political party behind them, while the writer may be an unknown speech writer. Public signs are authored by the government or institution that places the signs, but the writer is usually unknown. (A "No smoking" sign, for example, is authored by the government, but the writer is whomever designed the sign. People obey the authority of the government, not the authority of the sign maker.) We can consider the writer to be the speaker in the spoken mode. When you call your internet service provider to claim service under a warranty, you're only concerned with speaking with that author, i.e. the company, you normally don't care which particular speaker you talk to.

The division between author and writer can be unclear or the duties can be shared. A journalist is a writer in that he or she writes a newspaper article's words, but the author of those articles is both the journalist and his or her newspaper. When someone sues a newspaper for libel both the journalist and the newspaper may be sued as they are co-authors. A company is the author of an advertisement while the advertising agency is the writer. When controversy arises over the content of an advertisement, the company may attempt to place responsibility on the agency, but people are unlikely to be swayed, knowing as they do that the company authorised, and therefore authored, the offending advertisement.

In terms of the distinction between audience and reader, the **audience** is the ideal reader, that is, the receiver that the author and writer imagine when they produce the text. The **reader** is anyone who encounters the text, whether or not it was meant for him or her. Good writers will tailor their work to an idealised audience, making predictions about the audience's schematic knowledge, its cultural knowledge and questions it may have as it reads or listens to the text. Assuming the audience knows too little may cause boredom when the writer covers information that is unnecessary; assuming the audience knows too much may lead to confusion when the writer omits information he or she presumes the audience knows.

Magazines are usually quite clearly aimed at a specific audience. An article from the *FourFourTwo* football magazine begins as follows: "Liverpool and Arsenal shared the festive spoils in what proved to be a thrilling and open encounter at Anfield." The audience, those for whom this text is designed, will know that *Liverpool* and *Arsenal* are football teams and they will understand that *encounter* here is to be interpreted as "football match". Readers, those who come across the text, may not be able to interpret this, especially if they don't closely align with the ideal audience. What, for example, is the naïve reader to make of *Anfield*? They may guess that it is a place name, as it is preceded by *at* and begins with a capital letter, but they may be unaware that it is the home stadium of the team from Liverpool.

Exercise – register

The following email was sent to a linguistics discussion group as an answer to a question about phonology. Consider this email in terms of register. In all cases, identify words, phrases or clauses to support your answers.

1. What is the field of the text? Is the lexis field-specific or general?
2. What is tenor of the text? Does the author present himself as an authority or an equal?
3. What is the mode of the text? Does the text appear to be spontaneous or planned?

Subject: Re: phonology question

If it is a London thing, then the glottal stop which replaces the t in banter and the k in worker may be affecting the front end of the schwa vowel. I certainly noticed this when I was working at the school in Bermondsey, although it was more often a shortening of the schwa; the schwa was only lengthened when the -er word was a terminator. However, that was four years ago, and things move fast in teenage phonology. The devocalisation of the glottal stop was also sometimes carried over into the final syllable, so all you got was an exhalation or unvocalised h. It might be interesting to compare glottal-stopped words with words without a glottal stop, like hanger, banner, climber, etc.

Martin
(The Compleat Non-Phonologist)

Exercise – register (Commentary)

In Trudgill's terms, the topic of this email and the profession of its producer and receivers is indicated by the lexis: *syllable*, *vowel* and *phonology* all point to a discussion of language, particularly spoken language, by linguists. If we were to use Joos' conception of the five linguistic styles, consultative ("polite conversation", "two-way") might be the best choice. Although this is not spoken, we can see that it is like a two-way conversation, as we see reference to previous emails. (The *it* in "if it is a London thing" and the *the* in "the school in Bermondsey" both presuppose that readers will be able to interpret what is meant because they have read previous emails in this exchange.)

Neither the discussion of topic nor the categorisation of this email as one of five styles allows us to analyse the register as precisely as if we look at its field, tenor and mode. In terms of field, this is, as mentioned, a discussion of language, and in particular phonology. However, it is apparent that this is not a general discussion of language, but a highly specialised one. Words like *syllable*, *vowel* and *phonology* might be general terms understood by everyone, but *terminator*, *devocalisation* and *front end of the schwa vowel* are very low frequency, precise terms that are unlikely to be used in these senses outside of a discussion among those with specialist linguistic knowledge.

The tenor of this email is of particular interest, I think, because while the field is specialist, the tenor is somewhat informal. People sometimes assume that a precise discussion of an academic field must necessarily be formal, but that is not the case here. The writer uses an abbreviation (*etc.*). Some words he uses have more formal variants ("move fast" instead of "change rapidly" and "a London thing" instead of "a London-based phenomenon", for example). He does not address his readers ("Dear all", "Hello everyone", etc.) but simply begins writing about the topic in hand. This is not to be taken as rude, but simply reflects the ongoing nature of the discussion; the greetings have been done in an earlier email and are not needed again here. Similarly, he does not sign off with any formal expression ("Sincerely", "Thank you", etc.) and uses only his first name without any title or academic affiliation.

It is also notable that the producer presents himself as an equal in terms of tenor. His use of the precise language of the field means he is an expert, of course, but he shows us that he also considers his readers to be experts. He does not provide explanations of key concepts such as the phrase "the devocalisation of the glottal stop", assuming readers will already know them. If this was an email to students, he might have explained *glottal stop* to make sure they understood him, much as I did when I explained that term in Chapter 3. The writer hedges his claims ("may be affecting" instead of "is affecting") to show his awareness of the limits of his knowledge and he indicates that he may be wrong as his information is based on four-year-old data . He also calls himself a "Non-Phonologist", an additional way of underplaying his knowledge and signalling that he is not lecturing the expert readers, but is talking to them. Taken together, these indications of the tenor show us that not only is this a linguist writing to other linguists, but they are other linguists with whom he shares an ongoing relation of equality.

As far as the mode is concerned, this is clearly a written, planned email. The second sentence in particular, from "I certainly noticed…" to "terminator", is long and somewhat complex. There are no errors that suggest this was written in great haste. On the other hand, there are some indications of spontaneity, such as the aforementioned "London thing" and "all you got", which demand some interpretation by readers. In addition, the formatting of the email would likely be more varied in a completely planned text; perhaps by using italics and quotation marks to isolate linguistic terms under discussion. For example, part of the first sentence might be written as "…the glottal stop which replaces the *t* in 'banter' and the *k* in 'worker'…")

Genre

Discourses that share many features, including shared register, can be said to belong to the same **genre**, which Swales (1990) defines as texts which share a purpose. Thornbury (2005) provides a useful list of purposes to which most genres of discourse can be assigned.

1. referring – discourse designed to teach, including instructions manuals and lectures.
2. expressing – discourse designed to express emotions, likes and dislikes, including film reviews and gossip.
3. regulating – discourse designed to manage people's behaviour, including warning signs and election speeches.

4.   interacting – phatic discourse for the creation and maintenance of social relations, including dinner time chat with family and friendly conversations with friends and neighbours. (When I talk to my neighbour about all the spiders that have appeared in our gardens, we are mostly just talking for talk's sake. Neither of us are arachnologists with a particular interest in spiders and we are not worried about the spiders to the extent that we want to do anything about them. We are just talking to acknowledge each other. If he said "Hello" and mentioned the spiders and I did not respond we'd quickly fall out and no longer have a social relation.)

5.   playing – playful uses of language, including jokes and language games.

We are all familiar with genre in terms of thinking about the content of a text: the science-fiction genre features space travel and alien beings, the Western genre features cowboys and horses, and the romance genre features protagonists who must overcome obstacles to unite or reunite with their loved ones. Linguists use genre in this sense, but also to describe language use of other types that are not always thought of as being genres. A bus schedule, for example, has a referring purpose, as it's designed to teach us when the buses arrive and where they go. On the bus schedule affixed to a post near my home, the bus departure times are written in a vertical column while the bus stops are written horizontally across the notice. Some times are colour-coded to show that those buses only arrive on weekends. These are not necessary features of bus schedules, but they are quite common ones, and so can be said to be **genre conventions**, that is, features that typify a genre.

Cook (2011) lists the following as examples of genres: academic articles, news reports, advertisements, prayers, operas and menus. Think briefly of two features you might expect to see in each of those genres. If you can do so successfully you're doing a **genre analysis**, looking for common linguistic and non-linguistic features of those types of language use. When considering the opera genre, for example, you may be picturing singers in elaborate costumes, a non-linguistic feature, as well as the sung mode, a linguistic feature. For prayers you may think of the religious field of the prayers, a linguistic feature, and the (non-linguistic) body positions of the participants, whether they are clasping their hands together, bowing their heads, kneeling on the ground and so on. Any genre can be further subdivided into more specific genres, so menus, to take one example, may feature pictures and minimal text in fast-food restaurants, while menus in expensive, high-end restaurants typically don't have pictures, but do have elaborate descriptions of the ingredients ("organically-raised, locally-sourced beef") and the preparation process ("hand-cut vine-ripened tomatoes").

In Chapter 1 we looked at a recipe for chicken soup, the purpose of which was to inform readers about how to make that dish. Even if I hadn't said that it was a recipe, you would undoubtedly have known it was because you would have recognised many of the genre conventions. Some of those conventions are seen in the layout: a recipe usually has the item name at the top, a photograph of the food in its prepared form and a list of ingredients above the preparation instructions. Recipes in books by well-known chefs often feature a short introduction to the recipe at the top of the page: something about the best time of year to prepare the dish, a story about where the chef first learned the dish or an explanation of other foods that might be served to complement it. More straightforward recipes, such as those submitted to user-generated cooking websites, are less likely to display these features, moving directly to the list of ingredients without any preamble.

It is important to note that these genre conventions, and others like them, are just conventions. The organisation of these features is based on patterns that readers are comfortable seeing, but other patterns would be possible. A letter has the name of the writer at the end of the text, while a novel has the author's name at the start. Neither pattern is necessarily the best one, but we are used to them. A novel uses quotation marks to show character dialogue, but a comic book uses speech bubbles to show character dialogue.

The linguistic features that characterise a genre are more important in helping us determine its nature than conventions such as speech bubbles or the placement of photographs. If you saw something that was laid out like a recipe and featured a picture of food, but then read the text and saw the words "It was the best of times, it was the worst of times" and so on, you would, I think, be more inclined to believe that it was a strangely formatted version of Charles Dickens' *A Tale of Two Cities* than a recipe. It is the words of the text that are paramount in determining the genre.

Return to the example of the chicken soup recipe. In terms of field, a recipe is about food and cooking, so we will see many lexically cohesive terms related to both food (*oil, garlic, chicken*) and food preparation (*heat, pan, stir*). The lexis in that chicken soup recipe was quite general, but depending on the intended audience we might see words that were more specialised, such as *fricassee, santoku knife* and *julienne*, all of which would indicate an intended audience of people who were quite familiar with cooking.

In terms of tenor, a recipe is typically only semi-formal. On one hand, we probably don't expect slang, but on the other hand we probably don't have any strong expectations about whether or not a recipe should use contractions, phrasal verbs and other indications of informality.

Recipes are often only somewhat authoritative, treating readers as equals in terms of how much they are expected to know about cooking. (As we saw in Chapter 3, recipes typically feature the imperative mood, providing instructions.) Think of the ingredients list in a typical recipe. In some cases it will suggest quite precise measurements like "100 millilitres of oil" and "400 grams of chicken", which presents precise information in an authoritative manner. Other ingredients may be left more vague ("two large tomatoes" – How large is "large"?; "a pinch of salt" – How much salt is in "a pinch"?), which indicates that the producer expects the audience to have at least some prior experience in cooking. We can consider recipes to be a sub-genre of the instructions genre. We would expect other instructions to be much more precise. School science experiments or medical dosages don't typically assume equality, but instead present precise information with authority for fear that the experiment won't succeed or that the medicine will be harmful if too much or too little is taken.

The mode of a recipe is typically written and planned. As the recipe will be directed at an intended audience who know something about cooking, but not the specifics of this particular dish, the producer will want to provide enough necessary information without boring the reader with too many obvious details.

Too many changes to any of a recipe's linguistic features (the field, tenor, mode and the other genre conventions) would make the text appear to be part of a different genre. If we saw numerous declaratives ("The chicken was lightly fried") instead of imperatives ("Lightly fry the chicken...") we might be looking at a restaurant review instead of a recipe. If the mode was spoken instead of written, we might be listening to a cooking class. If the field was different, perhaps including words like *leg*, *headboard* and *screwdriver*, we might be reading instructions for the assembly of flat pack furniture.

Exercise – genre

Read the following article from *The Daily Mash* (http://www.thedailymash.co.uk/). Identify the genre conventions, make this appear to be a newspaper article. Identify the linguistic features that deviate from what we expect to see in the newspaper genre.

London property market based on people pretending grim places are great

30-05-13

A SHIT flat in London now costs £500,000 thanks to widespread delusion about whether a property is really depressing.

Inspiring

Property prices in the capital are rocketing as people behave like a structurally unsound ex-council flat in a post-industrial wasteland is a spectacular place to live.

34-year-old Emma Bradford said: 'I feel great about paying over £500k for a flat with no windows because it is quite near a Zone 12 train station, at least if I walk via the underpass – a journey with an impressive 34% survival rate.

'A cynical person could draw attention to the way some of the inner walls are made of cardboard but there are huge pluses like a bagel shop.'

Professor Henry Brubaker of the Institute for Studies said: 'Buying a place in London is a bit like organising a wedding – everything is absurdly expensive and not what you really want, but you just have to suck it up because it's all so bloody brilliant.'

Account executive Julian Cook said: 'When I visited a friend in Leicester last month, which of course is an absolute joke of a city, I couldn't help noticing their house had quite a lot of rooms in it.

'But how would I live without all the art galleries I never visit, my four-hour daily commute, being groped on the Tube, black snot, getting mugged for my iPhone, and my upstairs neighbour's regular all-night dubstep sessions?

'Hey wait – am I getting totally and utterly fucked over? Because my London estate agent seemed like a really great, honest guy.'

Exercise – genre (commentary)

The Daily Mash article's layout mimics conventional newspaper articles: there is a large-font headline at the top, the headline is written in the marked grammar of headlines (Note that it does not say "The London property market is based...", which would be grammatically complete.), there is a dateline below the headline, there is a medium-sized font subheading below the dateline, and there is a captioned photograph with the body of the text wrapped around it.

Within the body of the text, the article continues to resemble a newspaper article. The paragraphs are short, mostly just one sentence long. The clauses are mostly declaratives, as newspaper articles typically have a referring purpose. (Some newspaper articles, namely reviews, have an expressive purpose, while other such as opinion pieces have a regulating purpose as the author attempts to convince you to do something or believe something.) The article contains text written by the author and direct quotations from sources. Fairclough (1992, p. 104) calls these quotations **manifest intertextuality**, meaning that parts of other texts (*intertextuality*, or "relations between texts") are obvious to the eye (*manifest*) in the one being examined. A newspaper journalist would normally include quotations from reliable, authoritative sources to increase the authority of the article he or she is writing. The sources in this article are both people affected by the news ("34-year-old Emma Bradford") and experts commenting on the news ("Professor Henry Brubaker").

As is common in the satirical genre, for that is what this is, *The Daily Mash* article copies some of the conventions of the original genre, but manipulates others for effect. The swear words in the article are comical, because they would be highly unusual in conventional newspapers. (Much humour comes from seeing or hearing the unexpected.) The simple, uninformative name of the professor's "Institute for Studies" mocks the long, elaborate names of some academic institutes. The content of the article is, of course, the most obviously satirical element of this text. Newspaper journalists don't usually mock the homes, cities and economic decisions of those readers who might actually buy their newspapers. This satirical article has both a playful purpose, in that it is funny, but also a referring purpose, in that it comments on the absurdity of paying so much money for homes.

Chapter 5

Thinking about the Information

In this chapter we look at the information presented in discourse: how that information is organised, how certain information is highlighted in various ways using *discourse markers*, and how some information can left out of a text, yet understood to be present due to *implicature*.

———

Look at the following two short texts of the type I might use if I were to introduce myself to someone new.

5.1
A. I'm from Ottawa. The capital city of Canada is Ottawa.
B. I'm from Ottawa. Ottawa is the capital city of Canada.

Both A and B contain the same information: I say which city I'm from and I say that that city is the capital city of Canada. However, most people will think that either A or B is better than the other, although they may find it hard to explain why. Think for a few seconds about which is better-organised in terms of helping the discourse receiver follow what is being said.

   In my experience people tend to prefer B, saying that it seems to "flow better", "be more natural" and other similar comments. The only difference between the two is that the subject of the second sentence in A is *the capital city of Canada* while the subject of the second sentence in B is *Ottawa*, so it must be something about the information in these subjects that leads to the preference for B over A. Notice that subject of A, *the capital city of Canada*, does not mention information that was provided in the first sentence. However, the subject of B is the word *Ottawa*, which was previously mentioned. This repetition of *Ottawa* provides the link between the two sentences, leading us to see B as the more natural, better-organised pair of sentences.

Note that the actual word *Ottawa* does not have to be repeated. A personal reference, as discussed in Chapter 1, would also work, so C below feels just as natural as B.

5.2
C. I'm from Ottawa. It's the capital city of Canada.

It's not the direct repetition of the word that matters, it is the mention of previously given information that matters. When *it* is used, anaphorically presupposing *Ottawa*, we see the link between the two sentences, although we don't see *Ottawa* twice. Similarly in D below, where the subject is now *that city*, the demonstrative reference *that* in the subject *that city* points back to *Ottawa*, again making it clear that the two sentences are linked.

5.3
D. I'm from Ottawa. That city is the capital of Canada.

Furthermore, it is not necessary for the second sentence to begin with the **proper noun** *Ottawa* or a reference to *Ottawa* as the subject of the sentence. As long as *Ottawa* appears at the start of the second sentence, regardless of its grammatical function, people will be comfortable with the organisation of the two sentences. In the second sentence of E, *Ottawa* is now part of the prepositional phrase *in Ottawa*, while *people* is the subject. The two sentences continue to be clearly linked.

5.4
E. I'm from Ottawa. In Ottawa, people tend to speak both French and English.

Of course, the second sentence does not have to begin with *Ottawa* at all, or even mention *Ottawa* again. People would be equally comfortable with a sentence beginning with *I*, as in F, since *I* has also been previously mentioned.

5.5
F. I'm from Ottawa. I'm …

In F, it hardly matters what appears after *I'm* in the second sentence: my age, my job, my hobbies or anything else. As long as there is something at the start of the second sentence that provides a link to the previous sentence, people will see that the two are related.

The textual metafunction

In Chapter 2, we examined the *ideational metafunction* of language and discussed precise terms for expressing how language encodes different types of processes and participants. In Chapter 3, we examined the *interpersonal metafunction* and saw how we can describe the different ways language producers relate to language receivers.

The textual metafunction of language (Halliday, 2004), which is the third and final type, is its ability to show clear links between any new clause and the discourse that came before it. This metafunction explains how we organise information in clauses and show the connections between clauses. There are only two terms to remember in this discussion, **theme** and **rheme**, and the *theme* is the only one that matters in terms of describing those links.

Theme

The *theme* of a clause is its first linguistic element. It is the "point of departure" (Halliday, 2004, p. 89) of the clause. It is important to constantly remind oneself that in a discussion of theme in relation to the textual metafunction, the concern is only with this first linguistic element. *Theme* here does not mean "the main topic", "the key point" or anything else that we might associate with theme in other senses, including those definitions from literary studies, film criticism and so on.

In declarative clauses, the theme is often the subject of the clause, for this pattern of "subject first, then verb" is both simple and common in declarative clauses. In the following quotation from Winston Churchill, each clause begins with a subject which is also the theme: *I*, *dogs*, *cats* and *pigs*.

5.6
"I am fond of pigs. Dogs look up to us. Cats look down on us. Pigs treat us as equals."

Here we have seen a slightly more complex example of how themes provide links between clauses. Churchill's themes *dogs*, *cats* and *pigs* don't directly repeat information that came earlier in the first clause, which was what we saw in the examples related to *Ottawa* above. (Ignore Churchill's first theme, *I*, for a moment. We'll return to that.) However, we do see these four clauses as being linked. Why is that? In this case, the first clause "I am fond of pigs", although it is short, creates the possibility of a further elaboration on a number of topics: *I* (Churchill) might be mentioned next, providing further information about the speaker ("I grew up on a farm, so…"); *fond* might be discussed in detail, perhaps with an explanation of why he is fond of pigs or what other things he is fond of ("This fondness is…"); and *pigs* could be focused on for further discussion ("These animals…").

What we do see in the second clause is the theme *dogs*. *Dogs*, although not mentioned directly, are lexically cohesive with *pigs*, as they are collocations. A discussion of pigs can be thought of as being a discussion of animals generally, and domesticated animals more specifically, so it is not surprising to see *dogs* in the theme position when pigs have already been mentioned.

This is what we expect when we read or listen to a discourse that is well organised in terms of its thematic development. Themes of clauses will somehow relate to information that has been mentioned earlier, because themes contain "previously given" or "old" information. The third theme in the Churchill quotation is *cats*, which is lexically cohesive with *pigs* in the same way that *dogs* is, and is an even stronger collocation with *dogs* than *pigs*, as both are common pets. The theme of the fourth clause is *pigs*, which repeats previously given information, providing a clear indication that the clause it initiates is clearly linked to the previous three.

If we take snippets of other quotations from Churchill and place them one after the other, it is difficult or impossible to see any thematic development. Try to make sense of the following.

I am fond of pigs. Success consists of going from failure to failure without loss of enthusiasm. We shall fight on the beaches…

How does *success*, the theme of the second clause, possibly relate to the first clause? Were the pigs the ones that were successful? The third clause begins with the theme *we*, which is again hard to link meaningfully with what has come before. Are we to fight because he is fond of pigs? Are we to fight despite having gone from "failure to failure"? Most people would be comfortable saying that this example does not flow well and does not seem to have any natural connection. As a linguist, you can clearly say that the themes of the second and third clauses are not linked to what came before as they don't present old or previously given information.

The *rheme* of the clause is everything other than the theme. It is in the rhemes where new information appears. So the rhemes of the original quotation from Churchill are "am fond of pigs", "look up to us", "look down on us" and "treat us as equals". The rheme is the co-text of the theme that presents new information, which is linked to the earlier part of the discourse based on the link provided by the theme. In other words, the theme tells us how the message starts, then the rheme presents the rest of the message.

It is only in the first clause of any discourse that we can't see a link in the theme to the co-text, because of course there is no earlier co-text. When Churchill starts talking by saying "I am fond of pigs" we can't look back to see what earlier words the theme *I* is connected to, we can only see that *I* refers exophorically to the context, and thus that *I* here should be interpreted as referring to the speaker.

Note – marked and unmarked

The distinction between *marked*, a term I have used before, and *unmarked*, which I have avoided until now, is a useful one in many areas of linguistic study. *Marked* means "unusual" or "noticeably differently", while *unmarked* means "usual" or "normal". An American speaking English in America has an unmarked accent, as he or she sounds like the majority of people in that country, so we tend not to notice the accent or think about it. However, a British person who speaks English in America has a marked accent. People who hear the British accent may notice the difference. Of course the situation is reversed in Britain. Now it is an American who has a marked accent, but the British person's accent is unmarked.

These terms are useful because they allow us to discuss difference without necessarily saying that the difference is incorrect. It would be ridiculous to say that the British person's accent is wrong in America, but to say that his or her accent is marked allows us to indicate that something unusual has been noticed and may be worthy of discussion.

Markedness and unmarkedness don't only apply to accent, but can be applied to any linguistic concept where there exists more than one possibility. In English *you* as a pronoun is unmarked in terms of number, so it can mean either "one person" or "more than one person." This is sometimes confusing. Does "You should be quiet now" apply to only one child or to the whole class? This singular / plural ambiguity with *you* seems to have led to numerous informal marked plural forms of *you*: *you lot* (especially British), *you all* (especially American), *yinz* (Pittsburgh, Pennsylvania and environs) and so on.

Words can be considered marked and unmarked in terms of gender. A *tiger* or a *dog* is unmarked in terms of gender, referring to either a male or female. A *tigress* or a *bitch*, on the other hand, is always marked as female. (The *Kung Fu Panda* animated series character *Tigress* has a name that marks her as female, while other series characters like *Viper*, *Crane* and *Monkey* have unmarked names in terms of gender, although some are male and some are female.) If I say I saw *Arsenal* play football, people likely picture the men's team as *Arsenal* is the unmarked form of the name, although there is a women's team marked as the *Arsenal Ladies*. Similarly, the *PGA* is the men's "Professional Golfers' Association" (unmarked) while the *LPGA* is the "Ladies Professional Golf Association" (marked).

Some words are considered unmarked when they refer to women or female-gendered concepts. *Nurse* in its unmarked form is often taken to mean "female nurse", to the extent that you will sometimes hear people say "male nurse", indicating that they feel the sex of the nurse must be marked. It is not necessarily wrong to say "male nurse", but it is marked and thus worthy of further study. In the cases of *Arsenal, nurse* and so on, we might consider what marked and unmarked bits of discourse tell us about society's expectations of women's and men's jobs and roles.

Thus far, we have only been looking at theme in unmarked declaratives, that is, declaratives in which the subject comes first. However, other patterns are possible. In *marked declaratives* something other than the subject comes first.

5.7

A. "First they ignore you. Then they laugh at you. Then they attack you. Then you win." – Mohandas Gandhi, apocryphal

B. "Last night I dreamt I went to Manderley again." – *Rebecca*, Daphne du Maurier

C. "Little by little, one travels far." – JRR Tolkien, apocryphal

In A the theme of the first clause is the adverb *first*, which precedes the subject *they*. In B the theme is the adverb phrase *last night*, which precedes the subject *I*. In C the theme is the adverb phrase *little by little*, which precedes the subject *one*. These are thus all marked declaratives as their themes (the first element of the clause) are not their subjects. It is important to note that in any of these the clause could be rewritten to put the subject in the theme position: "They ignore you first", "I dreamt last night…" and "One travels far, little by little." As both the unmarked (subject first) and marked (subject not first) patterns are always possible, we should think about why the producer chose to do something unusual by using a marked theme.

Look again at A above, the quotation attributed to Mohandas Gandhi. The themes of the four clauses are *first*, *then*, *then* and *then*. *First* sets the theme of that clause as a time-ordered event. We are then not surprised to see further time-ordering devices, the temporal conjunction *then* in this case, in the following three clauses. The thematic development here is organised as a temporal sequence, highlighting the progression of these clauses as events that happen in specific times in relation to one another.

Other common marked themes in declaratives include marking for importance ("Most importantly, we see…", in which the theme is *most importantly* but the subject is *we*); adversity or opposition ("On the other hand, some have argued…", in which the theme is *on the other hand* but the subject is *some*); exemplification ("For instance, the first person to walk on the Moon said…", in which the theme is *for instance* but the subject is *the first person to walk on the Moon*) and manner ("Quietly, the door closed", in which the theme is *quietly* but the subject is *the door*).

Exercise – theme in declarative clauses

Read the following excerpt, which is adapted from a tour guide's description of London, given to tourists as they ride a bus through the city. Identify the themes and subjects of these clauses. Consider why the tour guide may have used marked themes in the places she did so.

```
01 Above us, you can see the sensational structure of these old
02 buildings. On the right you'll see Lock and Co, the oldest hat
03 maker in London. Directly in front of you there's the horse
04 guards coming up Piccadilly. Coming up on the left-hand side, the
05 Ritz Hotel is on the corner. If you fancy a great British
06 tradition you'll try afternoon tea at the Ritz. Also coming up,
07 these beautiful decorative gates were erected to commemorate
08 the ninetieth birthday of the Queen Mother.
```

Exercise – theme in declarative clauses (commentary)

As you see in the table below, most of the themes in this text are marked.

Marked theme	Subject
Above us (line 01)	you (line 01)
On the right (line 02	you (line 02)
Directly in front of you (line 03)	there (line 03)
Coming up on the left-hand side (line 04)	the Ritz Hotel (lines 04-05)
If (line 05)	you (line 05)
Also coming up (line 06)	these beautiful decorative gates (line 07)

Unmarked theme	Subject
you (line 06)	you (line 06 – unmarked theme)

Any of the clauses could have been spoken to put the subject first, but the tour guide marked certain specific information in the theme position. Most of the themes are related to directions: above us, on the right, and so on. The tour guide's register, specifically when we consider the tenor, shows evidence that she is the expert and the tourists are not. This text was not produced free of context, but instead is part of a discourse that includes the context of expert tour guide and naïve tourist. The guide first directs the tourists' attention to the location of the feature she wishes to describe in the theme of the clause, then provides new information in the rheme. In addition, the tour guide and the tourists are on a moving bus, which is also part of the context. If she doesn't direct their attention quickly, they'll have passed the sight before they've located it.

One sentence is different in that it contains two clauses, one with a marked theme and one unmarked. "If you fancy a great British tradition you'll try afternoon tea." This can be analysed in different ways, depending on the level of detail we think is needed to explain it. If we treat this as one sentence, the theme is the entire **dependent clause** "If you fancy a great British tradition" and the rheme is the entire **independent clause** "you'll try afternoon tea at the Ritz". (To distinguish between the two, remember that the dependent clause isn't enough on its own, so "if you fancy a great British tradition" doesn't seem to be complete because of the dependency marker *if*. The independent clause "you'll try afternoon tea" is complete on its own.) Here the tour guide does not thematise the directions, but instead thematises the conditionality ("if") of the information. Unlike the other clauses, which are presented as true for everyone ("you can see" (line 01), "you'll see (line 02)", etc.), the information in this rheme is only true on the condition of the theme, that is, only those who fancy tea will try it at the Ritz.

At another level of detail, we could analyse each of the two clauses in the sentence "If you fancy a great British tradition you'll try afternoon tea" on its own. The theme of the first clause is *if* while the subject is *you* (marked theme). The theme of the second clause is *you* and the subject is the same word, *you* (unmarked theme). This level of analysis is more precise as it is true that each clause has a theme and rheme. On the other hand, this level of analysis is not necessarily useful, as ultimately we will arrive at the same conclusion about the purpose of the thematisation of *if*, which is that it marks this clause as conditional, unlike the others that have no conditions. For the purposes of examining a text's overall organisation at the sentence level, rather than looking at the intricate relations between clauses within the sentences, it is often enough to look at the theme of each sentence rather than each clause.

Theme in interrogative and imperative clauses

Up to this point we have seen examples of themes, both unmarked and marked, in declarative clauses. Interrogative and imperative clauses also have themes which can be either marked or unmarked. If you understand the principles of theme and rheme in declarative clauses, it is relatively simple to apply your knowledge to clauses in a different grammatical mood.

Unmarked wh- interrogative clauses feature a wh- word in the theme position. These examples from song titles typify this pattern.

How soon is now? – The Smiths
Who wants to live forever? – Queen

Unmarked yes / no interrogative clauses feature a finite (*is, has, should,* etc.) followed by the subject. Further examples from song titles typify this pattern.

Do you really want to hurt me? – Culture Club
Should I stay or should I go? – The Clash (This is actually two clauses, both unmarked.)

Marked wh- interrogative clauses feature something other than the wh- word in the theme position. (The marked theme is less common, making it difficult to produce a list using song titles.)
Last night, where were you?
In that case what do you want to do?

Marked yes / no interrogative clauses feature something other than the finite+subject pattern. (Again, this pattern is less common, hence the lack of song titles in this realisation.)

Since last year have you been there?
With your good eyes can you see that sign on the building?

Unmarked imperative clauses begin with the verb.

Come as you are – Nirvana
Let's dance – David Bowie (Using *let's* with an imperative makes it an **inclusive imperative**, meaning both the producer and the receiver(s) are being prompted to do something.)

Marked imperative clauses begin with something other than the verb.

You be quiet. (Here the subject *you* is spoken, probably for emphatic purposes.)
When you get here, call me.

Patterns of organisation

There are two general patterns of thematic development that a text can follow (Danes, 1974). First, the theme of one clause can repeat the theme of a previous clause, providing further information about that same theme. Julius Caesar's letter to the Roman senate, describing a quick military victory, exemplifies this "fan" pattern, called so because the theme is the hub of the fan and the rhemes are the spokes.

Theme "I..." → Rheme 1 "...came."
→ Rheme 2 "...saw."
→ Rheme 3 "...conquered."

If we look again at the first three sentences of the Hillary Clinton speech we examined in Chapter 3, we see another example of this fan pattern. "Women comprise more than half the world's population. Women are 70 percent of the world's poor, and two-thirds of those who are not taught to read and write. Women are the primary caretakers for most of the world's children and elderly."

The word *women* appears in the text as the theme of three clauses, plus it is the elliptical theme of others. (The second sentence, for example, is interpreted as "Women are 70% of the world's poor, and [women are] two-thirds of those who are not taught to read and [women are two-thirds of those who are not taught to] write.") This fan pattern, with its repetition of the same theme, makes this passage particularly memorable, as with Martin Luther King Jr.'s repetition of the unmarked imperative theme ("Go back...") and Shakespeare's use of the marked interrogative theme ("If you..."), both of which we also saw in Chapter 3.

The second pattern, sometimes referred to as "zig-zag" pattern, sees part of the rheme of one clause become the theme of the next clause. In this pattern of thematic development the producer of the text moves from a general introduction to more specific detail. In the following example, notice how part of each rheme becomes the theme of the following clause. (The themes are in bold and the rhemes are in italics.)

I *am from Ottawa.*
Ottawa *is the capital of Canada.*
Canada *has several cities larger than Ottawa.*
Toronto, the largest city, *is home to several million people.*

The second and third themes are direct repetitions of a word from the previous rheme: *Ottawa* and *Canada*. The fourth theme, *Toronto, the largest city*, is not a direct repetition, but is an example of a "larger city", previously mentioned in the third rheme. (*Toronto, the largest city*, is a good example of **apposition**, where two noun phrases are placed side-by-side and both describe the same thing, but in different words. That's why both are taken as the theme here, not just *Toronto*.)

Exercise – patterns of thematic development

Read the following text, paying attention to the theme of each sentence. Identify any marked themes and explain how they help organise the text. Explain which pattern is most visible in each paragraph.

01 A bus crash in central Bolivia has injured more than 20 people. It only caused minor
02 injuries and bruises to most passengers, but several suffered head injuries. This was the
03 third such crash this year, officials reported.

04 A car was seen crossing the median between the lanes just prior to the crash. Witnesses
05 said the car appeared to be weaving awkwardly for several metres as it came along the
06 narrow road. The stretch of road is said to be notorious among locals for numerous
07 accidents.
08 Shortly after the accident police arrested the driver of the car. Officers said it is unknown
09 whether or not he was drinking prior to the incident.

Exercise – patterns of thematic development (commentary)

There is only one marked theme in this text. The theme *shortly after the accident* (line 08) is not the subject, *police*, thus it is marked. The first two paragraphs mostly describe events leading up to the accident ("a car was seen...", "witnesses said the car appeared..."), its immediate effects ("has injured...", "it only caused...") and general conditions related to this event ("this was the third...", "the stretch of road is said..."). *Shortly after the accident* frames the final paragraph as being a description of later events.

The first paragraph follows the fan pattern. The theme of the first clause, *a bus crash* (line 01), becomes *it* (line 01) in the second clause and *this* (line 02) in the third. Different words are used each time, but *it* (personal reference) and *this* (demonstrative reference) both refer to *a bus crash*. The second paragraph follows the zig-zag pattern. *Witnesses* (line 04) in the second clause provides further information about the rheme of the first clause, answering the question "A car was seen by whom?" The theme *the stretch of road* (line 06) gives specific information about one aspect of *the narrow road* (lines 05 and 06) mentioned in the previous rheme. (The first mention is of the road in general, the second is just of this particular stretch of it.) In the third paragraph the zig-zag pattern continues, with the theme *officers* (line 08) acting as a subordinate (officers are a type of police, hence subordinate) of information presented in the previous clause, *police* (line 08).

This is a relatively simple text for several reasons. Most obviously, it features high-frequency lexis known to everyone. The grammar is also quite simple, with most sentences containing only one or two clauses. Less obviously, the thematic development is quite simple. Themes are mostly unmarked and each paragraph follows the fan or zig-zag pattern. More complex texts may feature a mix of patterns within one paragraph, in which one theme refers to the previous theme and the next one refers to a previous rheme. In addition, more complex themes may reach further back in the text, developing old or previously given information from several clauses or paragraphs back. Themes don't have to develop information from sentences just before; they can reach back quite far. However, if a writer or speaker starts to develop a theme from too far back in a text, listeners or readers may fail to see the connection.

Types of theme

To be precise, we can further subdivide themes into three types: topical, textual and interpersonal themes.

Topical themes are those which relate to the content ("topic") of the text that comes before them. These are the themes that, for the most part, I have been explaining thus far, although for the sake of simplicity I have simply called them *themes* rather than *topical themes*. If we return to the first two clauses of *Patterns of thematic development* exercise, we see it begins with the following two clauses: "A bus crash in central Bolivia has injured more than 20 people. It only caused minor injuries and bruises to most passengers, but several suffered head injuries." Here it is apparent that the theme of the second clause, *it*, is clearly linked to the previous clauses because the personal reference *it* refers to the same topic as the first, "a bus crash in central Bolivia". Many themes develop in this fashion, by including information that was given earlier in the text. This makes it clear to receivers that the new clause is connected to the previous ones.

A **textual theme** provides a link, usually in the form of a conjunction, between the clause it initiates and the clause before it. Look at the conjunctions in the following example. "Why do I like cycling? It's cheaper than a car. Next, cycling is faster than walking. Then it's also better for my health." The two temporal conjunctions, *next* and *then*, are used as themes to show that the speaker is presenting a list of reasons. *Next* and *then* situate the clauses they initiate as being part of a list, but these themes alone do not explain how these clauses are related to the *topic* of what has come before. We still need the topical theme to see that link. (If you only heard "It's cheaper than a car. Next...", you would assume that a related topic would follow *next*, but you couldn't be sure.) We can present the underlined themes of the second, third and fourth clauses like this.

"Why do I like cycling? <u>It's</u> cheaper than a car. <u>Next</u>, <u>cycling</u> is faster than walking. <u>Then</u> <u>it's</u> also better for my health."

It = topical theme. *It* presupposes "cycling", so the clause that follows is related to the topic.
Next = textual theme. The clause that follows is part of a list.
cycling = topical theme. The clause that follows is related to the topic.
Then = textual theme. The clause that follows is part of a list.
it = topical theme. *It* presupposes "cycling", so the clause that follows is related to the topic.

The textual theme is often optional. You could remove *next* and *then* from the example and still expect people to understand. The topical theme is not optional. If listeners did not hear a theme that is related to the topic of what came before, they would be unsure if the new clause was related to the previous ones.

An **interpersonal theme** shows how the clause it initiates is related to the listeners or readers. Here we will usually see vocatives (see Chapter 1), which tell us which person or people the clause is directed at, question words, or the finite of the verb (Chapter 3) that is used to form a question. If a reading teacher says "Children, open your books. Roshana, read the first page, please", the words *children* and *Roshana* are interpersonal themes that show who the clauses are directed at. The words *open* and *read* are topical themes that show a relation to the topic of reading. If the teacher were then to ask the class "Do you like this book?" we would see the interpersonal theme *do*, which indicates the teacher is relating this clause to the children as a question, followed by the topical theme *you*, which is related to the topic of the class, that is, children ("you") learning to read.

Exercise – topical, textual and interpersonal themes

A clause can have more than one type of theme. Identify the themes in Macie's utterance in line 02. Think about how Macie's first few words initiate her turn and orient her answer to the content of the discussion (the topical theme), to the previous clause (the textual theme) and to her listener, Sybilla (the interpersonal theme).

```
01 Sybilla: Let's swim with Tillie tomorrow.
02 Macie:   But Sybilla, she is going to be away.
```

Exercise – topical, textual and interpersonal themes (commentary)

Macie's response in line 02 helps orient her clause to Sybilla's clause in several ways.

But = textual theme. This adversative conjunction shows that this clause has an adversative relationship with the one that came before. ("You, Sybilla, want to swim. My clause will show a problem with that.")
Sybilla = interpersonal theme. This shows that the clause to follow is addressed to Sybilla, not to anyone else who may be listening.
she = topical theme. Finally we see how the topic of this clause relates to the clause that came before. *She* is a personal reference that presupposes *Tillie*, which is given information as *Tillie* has been previously mentioned.

Note that once we reach *she*, the theme is finished. This clause has now been oriented to the text, the listener and the topic. Anything that follows is the rheme, which could contain any new information, as in the following examples.

```
01 Sybilla: Let's swim with Tillie tomorrow.
02a Macie: But Sybilla, she doesn't know how to swim.
02b Macie: But Sybilla, she said she doesn't want to.
02c Macie: But Sybilla, she needs a new swim costume.
```

Discourse markers

In the course of your daily life you will sometimes see a person walking alone and purposefully in one direction, then suddenly turn around and walk equally as purposefully in the other direction. If you're a keen observer and listener, as all discourse analysts should aim to be, you may have noticed that this sudden about-face is often accompanied by the utterance "oh". This little sound, and others like it, is sometimes dismissed as "filler", meaningless noise that is not important in terms of thinking about how language works. And yet, if we recognise that people make conscious decisions, albeit very quick ones, when they speak, *oh* can't be dismissed. We think about what we want to say, we decide on the sounds needed to say it, and we use our vocal folds (also known as vocal cords), tongue, lips and teeth to make those sounds. This admittedly brief and simplistic description of speech production should be kept in mind whenever we think about language use. People consciously choose to say things, and thus nothing should be considered meaningless.

Returning to *oh*, we would likely think that a person who spins around and walks off in another direction while saying "oh" has just realised something: perhaps he forgot his keys, maybe she decided she didn't have time to walk home and decided to take the bus, and so on. The bit of spoken text, "oh", in combination with the context, the person's about-face, allows us to analyse the discourse as representing a situation in which the speaker has suddenly discovered some new information. As Schiffrin says (1987, p. 74), "*oh* occurs as speakers shift their orientation to information". The speaker marks the discovery of new information ("I forgot my keys", etc.) with "oh", despite the fact that the new information was only in his or her head.

We, bystanders to the person's internal and spoken discourse, recognise this discovery of new information much more readily when we hear "oh" than if it was not spoken. If we see a person make a 180° turn and walk off without hearing "oh", we have less to work with and so can't be as sure of the reason for the turn. Perhaps the person had reached the point where her morning walk ends and thus turned as planned; she didn't just discover the need to turn, it was previously established in her mind, and thus was not marked with "oh". Perhaps the person is simply an eccentric, turning and turning again without feeling the need to signal his decisions to do so as newly discovered information. And, of course, perhaps he or she did just realise that the house keys were in fact still in the office, but did not mark this discovery with "oh". We make conscious decisions, after all, and so don't have to verbalise our discoveries.

Oh is a discourse marker. The definition of discourse marker is contentious, as is the choice of what to count or not count as examples of such. For my purposes, Fung and Carter (2007, p. 418), who expanded on the work of Maschler (1994), provide a definition that is both comprehensive and clear. For them, discourse markers "are defined as intra-sentential and supra-sentential linguistic units which fulfil a largely non-propositional and connective function at the level of discourse. They signal transitions in the evolving process of the conversation, index the relation of an utterance to the preceding context and indicate an interactive relationship between speaker, hearer, and message." This means they can occur within sentences ("intra-sentential") or between sentences "supra-sentential"), they don't change the "true or false" meaning of their co-text ("non-propositional"), and they make links between the speaker, the listener and the text.

More succinctly, but less precisely, discourse markers somehow "mark" the surrounding discourse in one way or another. Fung and Carter (2007) provide a list of four ways in which this marking of discourse occurs: referential, interpersonal, structural and cognitive. Although Fung and Carter were describing the functions of discourse markers in pedagogic discourse, that is, discourse related to teaching and learning, their four functions are broadly applicable to other forms of discourse. (It should also be noted that discourse markers, while commonly associated with speaking, are used in written discourse, although some of the less formal markers such as *oh*, *like* and *well* are more common in speech.)

Referential discourse markers

These discourse markers indicate a relationship between the co-text that precedes them and the co-text that follows them. These discourse markers were previously discussed as *conjunctions* in the discussion of cohesion in Chapter 1, so we already have useful meta-language to discuss these relationships: additive, adversative, causal and temporal. Consider the following brief exchange.

5.9

```
01 Parent:      have you written that card yet
02 Child:       i don't want to
03 Parent:      but you have to
```

Here the conjunction *but* functions as a discourse marker, as it marks the parent's turn in line 03 as existing in an adversative relationship with the child's turn in line 02. The child must write the card despite not wanting to.

Notice that we might still interpret this adversative relationship between turns 02 and 03 without the discourse marker. The child's "I don't want to" followed by the parent's "You have to" makes sense as a contradiction by the parent, especially if we see the parent's stress on "have" as providing further evidence of contrast between the two turns. This is because discourse markers are usually defined as being **detachable**, meaning they can be removed from the text without changing its propositional meaning and without making the text ungrammatical. However, the understanding of the discourse without the discourse marker may force us to rely more heavily on using context. Without *but* in the text, we still have the parent's status as an authority figure to help us interpret the relationship between turns 02 and 03. The presence of *but* makes that relationship clearer. As Fraser (1999, p. 938) argues, discourse markers "impose a relationship between some aspect of the discourse segment they are a part of, call it S2, and some aspect of a prior discourse segment, call it S1". *But* forces the child to see the parent's imposition of an adversative relationship between turn 03 (what Fraser calls S2) and turn 02 (what Fraser calls S1).

Other referential discourse markers include *because* (and the less formal *coz*), *or*, *so* and the other terms named in Chapter 1 as *conjunctions*. I'm not now asking you to disregard the description of them as conjunctions; these words are generally discourse markers, but more specifically they are conjunctions, one type of discourse marker.

Note – verbal operator do

As discussed in Chapter 1, *do* in all of its forms (*does*, *did*, etc.) is sometimes a verbal substitute, as in the case of "My cousin races on Saturday and Sunday, but I just do on Sunday with him." Here *do* is interpreted as "race." *Do* can also be a lexical verb meaning "perform" or "complete", as in "Do your piano lesson before dinner." (The *do* in the *Star Wars* character Yoda's exhortation "Do or do not. There is no try" is also a lexical verb *do*.)

A third function of *do*, the verbal operator, is to turn declarative clauses into their interrogative, negative or emphatic forms.

1. "We go to bridge." – declarative clause
2. "Do we go to the bridge?" – *Do*'s function is to make the clause interrogative.
3. "We don't go to the bridge." – *Do*'s function is to make the clause negative, giving us something to attach *not* to. (We don't normally hear "We not go to the bridge" unless we are talking to cavemen.)
4. "We do go to the bridge." – *Do*'s function is to make the clause emphatic. (See Chapter 3 for a discussion of the finite being used for emphasis.)

Interpersonal discourse markers

These discourse markers may indicate something about the speaker's attitude towards the text and the listener's probable attitude towards it. The speaker who initiates a turn with the discourse marker *obviously*, as in "Obviously we can't go now that you're sick", may wish to indicate that the co-text following "obviously" is not meant to belittle the listener's intelligence. Simply marking the co-text as *obvious* both indicates the speaker's attitude towards it and projects the listener's attitude towards it. Other discourse markers with this interpersonal function include *you see*, *really*, *actually* and *to be honest*. The oft-maligned discourse marker *you know* also falls in this category. First, consider *you know* in excerpt 5.1, which is not a discourse marker.

Excerpt 5.10

```
01 C:    you know my neighbour
02 V:    yeah the smo/ker
03 C:    yeah
```

In excerpt 5.10, C has omitted the **verbal operator** *do* from her words, but V (line 02) has interpreted line 01 as the question, "Do you know my neighbour?", hence the response "yeah" and the offer of more precise identification, "the smoker". This "you know" is clearly a subject and a verb. In excerpt 5.11, however, neither instance of *you know* from B (lines 02 and 05) is treated as a question by either of the participants (B is an employee and M is the manager. They are discussing their coffee shop's new advertising campaign.)

Excerpt 5.11

```
01 M:    it's quite fun this advertisement
02 B:    it's quite fun but it's <..> that <.> you know a very <.>
03       unique advertisement as well
04 M:    normally <.> coffee shops never do advertisements like this
05 B:    yeah it's quite unique and eye-catching so <..> you know <.>
06       it's just to catch the attention of customers
```

Here B appears to be tentative about expressing her opinion. We see her repeat her manager's word in line 02, which is a common way that we show agreement, but we also see a false start (line 2 "that") and numerous pauses throughout her turns, which are both often signs of disfluency in spontaneous speech. (In planned spoken discourse, such as a politician's speech, pauses might be used for effect.) Furthermore, she twice says *you know*, but neither seems to be interpreted as a question, as we don't see M respond to either of them. Perhaps because M is the manager, someone with more authority and more experience, B wishes to avoid presenting herself as a lecturer, something that could cause offense. The interpersonal discourse marker *you know* helps minimise the strength of her declarations by making it clear that she thinks her manager already knows what she is saying. As she speaks B is saying what she wants to say while simultaneously projecting herself into her manager's role, then marking her speech with *you know* to avoid making it appear that she thinks her manager is ignorant.

You know is little different from more elaborate constructions, such as "As I am sure you are aware...", which also seek to avoid causing offence by prefacing what might be seen as evident information. The function of the two is similar, but the form is different. Linguistic prescriptivists would not likely criticise "As I am sure you are aware...", but *you know* is commonly thought to be an indication of slovenly speech and a lazy mind. A descriptive linguist would call *you know* informal and would recognise its effective role as a marker of shared knowledge.

Structural discourse markers

Texts, whether written or spoken, have structure, by which is meant "typical patterns of organisation": stories are often organised chronologically, business plans may be written as a problem with a proposed solution, instructions for assembling a child's toy are presented as sequential steps, and so on. Kaplan (1966) started an ongoing discussion in linguistics, and especially in teaching English as a second or foreign language, about whether typical text structures are common to all people, or are products of our individual cultures. There is still some debate over the answer, but we can agree that when people read or hear a text that is not well organised, they may find it difficult to understand or even reject paying further attention to the text, thinking that it is nonsense.

When a teacher tells students they should write a paragraph by indenting it or leaving a line space, starting with a topic sentence, adding supporting details, and so on, the students are being introduced to the conventions of text structure. In written texts, structure is often clearly marked using orthography (capital letters for new sentences, punctuation), fonts, coloured text, photographs and other visual aids. A newspaper article has a bold headline in a large font at the top of the page, photographs have captions in yet another font that help distinguish them from the main text, and paragraphs are typically only one or two sentences long, which is said to help make articles easier to read.

The structure of a written text is also signalled through the words used. Clear discourse markers such as *first* (or more formally *firstly*), *second* (*secondly*), *then* and *finally* make it clear that the writer is enumerating points in sequence, for example. These adverbs are also used when speaking, but there are numerous other discourse markers that help organise spoken texts, which is important because speakers can't rely on fonts, punctuation, etc. to structure their texts. In excerpt 5.12 a plumber introduces a DIY video. Look at the words *okay* (line 01) and *so* (line 02) and think about how each helps to organise the discourse here.

```
Excerpt 5.12
01 Okay in today's video we're going to talk about how to replace
02 or install a wash basin. So what we've got here today is a very
03 very small sink that we're going to change over for this lovely
04 pedestal.
```

Okay (line 01) is commonly used in positions like this, to start a new discourse or new topic. This is clearly not the *okay* used synonymously with *yes* to answer questions, as no question has been asked. This *so* (line 02) is used to mark a shift in the topic from the general introduction of what viewers will learn in the video to the more specific case of the small sink that will be used as an example. This *so* is clearly not an **intensifier** used to add force ("It's so cold"), nor is it a causal conjunction.

We can't dismiss *okay*, *so* and other structural discourse markers (*right*, *now*, *yeah*, etc.) as meaningless, as some critics tend to do. These words are used very consistently in similar places and so do have meaningful roles in organising discourse, although they may not be the formal uses of the words that we might expect to see listed first in dictionaries. Thorne (2008) explains that written language has historically been considered the more prestigious mode of language, so we tend to draw our notions of what standard English is from written forms. Spoken forms, though perhaps less formal, function with equal purpose. It is because they are considered non-standard forms or even meaningless fillers that books on language tend to spend so much time explaining them.

Cognitive discourse markers

Some discourse markers are used to comment on the speaker's thinking process. We use *well* to mark upcoming discourse as recently decided ("Well, since you've explained it so clearly, I can't refuse"); *I think* to show that we are either hesitant or conclusive about our thoughts (consider the difference between a tentative "I think it will be okay" with the stress on *think*, and a more authoritative, argumentative "I think you're wrong" with stress on *I*); *I mean* when we want to rephrase or elaborate, and so on.

Fung and Carter (2007) also include *like* as an example of a discourse marker that marks elaboration in the speaker's discourse. *Like* is very **productive**, meaning it appears in new forms more than other words, to the extent that prescriptivists commonly complain about its overuse. (Note that *like* was one of the banned words discussed in Chapter 3.) People who criticise *like* may be confusing the word's **form**, meaning its appearance, with its **function**, meaning its purpose. The following examples of *like* have the same form, but function differently. (Fuller (2003) provides a thorough explanation of several functions of *like*.)

5.13
1. I like you. (lexical verb – "have positive feelings for")
2. Mr Rose dances like a snake. (preposition – "similar to")
3. The driver was like slow down. (quotative *like* – Used in place of *say* to quote words or a summary of the original words. Also use to quote emotional states, as in "I was like angry.")
4. He was like 25 years old. (discourse marker – "looseness of meaning." Used to indicate that the following may be approximate.)
5. We've got to meet by like 6 or we can't make it. (discourse marker – "focus." Used to indicate that the following is particularly important. This "6" is unlikely to be approximate as the speaker explains why the time is important in the second clause "or we can't make it.")

Like as a verb or preposition does not irritate people, but the quotative and discourse marker functions do tend to, probably because of the **speaker variable**, namely age (young), that is associated with those functions.

Exercise – discourse markers

In the following conversation two employers, *I* and *P*, discuss work with their employee, Alex (*A* in the transcription), a music DJ. Identify the types of the underlined discourse markers, then explain the function of those discourse markers.

```
01 I:   so <.> alex <.> we've gathered here <.> because we wanted to
02      talk to you about dj'ing the festival
03 A:   yeah
04 I:   er <.>
05 P:   like we're gonna make your job easier
```

Exercise – discourse markers (commentary)

I introduces the new topic with "so" (line 01), a structural discourse marker, then shows that the first clause of line 01 ("we've gathered here") is the cause of the second clause ("we wanted…") with "because", a referential discourse marker. In line 03 *A* indicates he is listening with "yeah", an interpersonal discourse marker. This "yeah" shouldn't be seen as an indicator of polarity (see Chapter 1), as A is not answering a question. In line 04 *I* marks his thinking process with "er", a cognitive discourse marker. Discourse markers like this allow a speaker to attempt to **hold the floor**, that is, to indicate that he or she wishes to continue speaking. (When we want to talk but are prevented from doing so, perhaps because we are eating or coughing, we sometimes hold up a hand to indicate that we wish to hold the floor.) After *I* pauses in line 04, *P* begins her turn in line 05 with "like", a cognitive discourse marker that shows her turn is an elaboration on *I*'s turn in lines 01 and 02. We can see turn 05 as an elaboration because it answers the unspoken question "What do we want to talk to you about?" that was raised by *I* in turns 01 and 02.

Notice that the conversation would be comprehensible, albeit somewhat stiff, even if the discourse markers were removed.

I: "Alex, we've gathered here. We wanted to talk to you about dj'ing the festival."
P: "We're gonna make your job easier."

The discourse markers do not change the propositional meaning of what was said, but they do give us more information about how the speakers relate to the discourse and the connections they see between its different parts.

Implicature

In the introduction to this book, I asked you to make sense of my daughter saying "I'm hungry", which I argued meant "Feed me." This can be described in linguistic terms. *I* is a first-person pronoun being used as a subject, as opposed to *me*, which is a first-person pronoun used as an object. The next bit, *'m*, is a contraction of the verb *am*, which is the verb *be* in the present tense, simple aspect. *Hungry* is an adjective in the complement position that tells us something about the subject *I*. (Normally we may think of adjectives as modifiers that appear before nouns, as in the children's book title *The Very Hungry Caterpillar* by Eric Carle, but here *hungry* appears in a different position, so it's called a complement, although it does the same job in that it gives more information.) This is a simple explanation of "I'm hungry", but that grammatical explanation doesn't do much to tell us what she means when she says it.

My daughter's words mean something other than what she said, so in linguistic terms she has created an **implicature**, an implicit meaning that differs from the words spoken. Her bit of text, "I'm hungry", exists as part of a discourse which includes our parent–child relationship, so the implicature "Feed me" is understood by us and by anyone who is aware of typical parental duties. (*Implicature*, a noun, is related to the verb *imply* and the noun *implication*. However, as *imply* and *implication* are widely used in non-linguistic discourse to mean various other things, it is best to use *implicature* as the noun and *implicate* or *create an implicature* as the verb when discussing this linguistic concept.)

The concept of implicature is associated with Grice (1975), who explained how we could describe implicature by realising that people follow a **cooperative principle** when they interact. Grice (1975, p. 45) described the principle like this: "Make your conversational contribution such as is required, at the stage at which it occurs, by the accepted purpose or direction of the talk exchange in which you are engaged." Whether we are producing or receiving language, we do not only focus on the words, which would be uncooperative. We instead realise that those words exist in a certain context (time, place, relationship), and we cooperate to interpret what we receive as discourse and expect our receivers to also interpret what we produce as discourse.

The concept of implicature helps us describe what is happening in exchanges such as the following:

```
5.14
01 M: where's my book bag
02 S: it must be somewhere
```

M's question in line 01 would seem to demand that *S* either answer with the location of the book bag, or say, "I don't know." If we only consider the words in *S*'s answer in line 02, they do not appear to contribute anything to the exchange. Of course the book bag "must be somewhere"; it is impossible for it to be nowhere. However, if we assume that *S* is cooperating with *M*, as least minimally, we might see line 02 as creating the implicature "Keep looking." Perhaps *M* and *S* have had similar exchanges before, in which case we might interpret the implicature in line 02 as "You always lose things. I'm not helping again." We, as outsiders, cannot always determine precisely what the implicature might be because we are not part of the same context as these speakers, so our interpretations may differ from theirs.

If I phone my wife twice in rapid succession, she sometimes says "You again" after she's identified me in the second call. Why would she say something so obviously true? Her phone's caller identification feature identifies my name when it rings and she knows my voice when I speak. Her implicature might be "Good, I'm glad you've called again" or perhaps "Why are you bothering me again?", depending on whether I am in her good books at the time or not.

Grice (1975) explained that we seem to follow rules when we cooperate to communicate with others. He called these *maxims*, meaning "linguistic rules of conduct that we tend to follow"; they are not rules that we must follow. These four maxims are often called **Grice's maxims** (or *Gricean maxims*), as they are so clearly connected with Grice's work. According to the cooperative principle, when we interact in speech and writing we assume people are following these four maxims:

1. The maxim of quantity: give the proper amount of information
2. The maxim of quality: try to say only what is true
3. The maxim of relevance: make what you say relevant to the topic at hand
4. The maxim of manner: avoid ambiguity or obscurity, be brief and orderly

To **adhere** to the maxims is to follow them, doing as is expected. To **violate** the maxims is to break them, but without expecting others to know why we are doing so. To **flout** the maxims is to break them, but for reasons we expect others to understand. The information that we expect others to understand when we flout the maxims is the implicature.

Quantity – When an acquaintance asks "How are you?" you probably say "Fine" or some other short answer. When a doctor asks you a similar question you probably give a more detailed answer, mentioning recent health problems that you wouldn't have told the acquaintance. In both cases you are adhering to the maxim of quantity, that is, the right amount of information you should give at this time in order to be cooperative. Giving an acquaintance too many details about your poor health might be seen as embarrassing or as a request for sympathy. Giving the doctor too little information wouldn't give him or her enough detail to possibly help you.

Quality – I am 44 years old now. If you ask me my age and I tell you that I am 44 I am adhering to the maxim of quality, that is, I am telling the truth. We are both cooperating as we have both acted as we expect each other to act when a question is asked. If you ask me my age and I tell you that I am 43 or 45, I do not think you would know that I am not telling the truth. The age difference is slight, so I would probably successfully trick you into thinking I was something other than 44 years old. In this case I would be violating the maxims, but there would be little else to say about this in terms of cooperating, as this lie would only benefit me. Perhaps I want to appear slightly younger or older for some reason. (The difference between 43 and 44 may be largely insignificant, but young people who lie about their age in order to purchase alcohol or see a film that is age-restricted are violating this maxim with a clear purpose.) If you ask me my age and I say something like "Not as old as you think", I am flouting the maxim. I've given you an answer that you can interpret, so I am not violating the maxim, but it is not the true answer, so I am not adhering. You would probably think that I did not want to tell you my age, the implicature being something like "Don't ask me my age, as it suggests you think that I am old."

Relevance – We flout the maxim of relevance when we say things that do not appear to be related to what came before until we consider the context. When the telephone rings in my house we sometimes hear an exchange like the following.

```
5.15
01 G: phone <.> I'm washing dishes
02 S: okay
```

The first TCU ("phone") in *G*'s turn in line 01 draws attention to the phone. We do not normally call out names of household electronics, so hearers will realise that this utterance must be relevant to the context and means "The phone is ringing." The second TCU in line 01 ("I'm washing dishes") indicates that *G* cannot answer the phone herself, as her hands are wet. Taken together, this turn creates the implicature "Someone answer the phone." Notice that *S* in line 02 answers the implicature and agrees to answer the phone; he reacts to what *G* means, not just to the words she says. If *G* were to fully explain what she meant in her first turn, we would probably think she was violating the maxim of quantity. It would seem odd for her to say "The phone is ringing. We answer the phone when it rings. Someone must do so, but I cannot because my wet hands would possibly damage the phone. Therefore, someone else must do so."

Manner – This maxim appears to be the catch-all category for linguistic behaviour that is not accounted for by the other maxims. The most well known example of flouting the maxim of manner is demonstrated when adults spell out words to avoid having young children understand them. A child's father who says "Someone S-T-O-L-E that thing she rides on. What should we tell her?" to the child's mother is, at first glance, not being brief (Why spell the word *stole*?) and is being unnecessarily ambiguous (Is "that thing she rides on" a scooter, a bicycle or something else?) However, within the family context the mother will understand that implicature "Someone stole her bicycle" and will understand that the father says this to avoid making the child sad or worried.

Some explanations of the four maxims become mired in discussion of which maxim or maxims we should be looking at when we think about a particular spoken utterance or written expression. It is probably best, at least at first, to focus instead on deciding what the implicature is. It is also interesting to think about why speakers flout to create an implicature rather than simply adhering to the maxims, but we can't always be certain of their reasons as we are not privy to their thoughts.

Exercise – Grice's maxims

In the following examples, identify the implicature that has been created. (Note that your answers may differ depending on the contexts you envision.)

1. A child is reaching touch a pot. Her parent says "That's hot."
2. A parent asks a child who is leaving the house "Where are you going?" The child says "Out."
3. A man returns late from a trip to the supermarket and says "There were thousands of people so it took a while."
4. Stevie Wonder sings "You are the sunshine of my life."

Exercise – Grice's maxims (commentary)

1. The implicature is "Do not touch that pot." Saying "That's hot." provides a reason for the implicature. With very young children a parent might adhere to the maxim and simply say "Don't touch that."
2. The child is flouting if it is evident that he or she is moving to go out of the house. Saying "Out" creates an implicature akin to "I don't want to tell you specifically where I am going" or "It is not your business." A parent may react negatively to this

implicature, feeling that the parent-child context demands an answer that adheres to the maxims and provides a full explanation.

3. Unless there were in truth "thousands of people" in the supermarket, an unlikely situation, we should see that the man is creating the implicature "The supermarket was crowded." This use of **hyperbole**, an exaggeration for emphatic purpose, was perhaps done to give a reason for his lateness.

4. No matter how much Mr. Wonder loves someone, that person cannot literally be sunshine. This is a **metaphor**, so the connotations of sunshine (warm, pleasant, bright) are implicated as being qualities of the subject of the song.

Extended analyses

A common feature of books such as the one you are reading is their tendency to look at linguistic features and concepts in isolation. Metafunctions, maxims, modality and so on are explained and exemplified in various sequences, but without much attention being paid to showing the links between these concepts. This is for two reasons, I think. First, it is probably easiest to understand a particular concept by studying it by itself, without the possible confusion that may arise from studying two or more concepts at the same time. In reality, all the different concepts discussed in this book are present at the same time. The field of a text affects the author's stance, as we may speak or write more confidently about topics we are familiar with. If I were to try to explain how a car works, a topic about which I know little, you would hear more epistemic modality in my language: "This *might* be the carburettor", "*I think* these are spark plugs", and so on. The tenor of the conversation would similarly affect my stance. I think I use more tentative language, and thus more deontic modality, when I talk with my boss: "We *might* introduce a new class…", "*Perhaps* you *should* ask students to…" and so on.

Second, space limitations preclude a full discussion of any bit of discourse being analysed. Authors choose excerpts from novels, conversations or other texts, explain how the concept being analysed appears in those excerpts, then move on to the next topic. If I were to present whole texts every time I chose an example, rather than specific excerpts, the size of this book would quickly become unmanageable. The examples you read herein are thus presented without their accompanying co-text and without the accompanying context. When I say "Imagine a teacher tells her class that 2+2 equals 4", I am asking you to pretend that the co-text is relevant to a mathematics lesson and that the context is a classroom, but the real co-text is the words in this book and the context is the book itself and whatever situation you are reading it in, perhaps for pleasure, or perhaps because you were instructed to.

Exercise – analysing discourse

In order to try to overcome these limitations, the following section presents two longer extracts of texts that you can use to practise your analytic skills. The first, a written text, is an excerpt of a fairy tale called *The Dragon Rock*, by Ellena Ashley. (The full text is available online at http://www.eastoftheweb.com/short-stories/UBooks/DragRock.shtml.) The second, a spoken text recorded by Bansri Kakkad, is a transcription of a conversation between a hairdresser and a customer. For both texts, look at them as products of discourse, that is, texts that were created by specific authors, for specific audiences, at specific times and places, and for specific purposes. Consider how these contextual factors influence the text. You may want to consider the texts using any of the concepts discussed in this book. A limited commentary follows each text, although you may find you have other ideas than those presented in the commentaries.

The Dragon Rock by Ellena Ashley

This story begins with Once Upon A Time, because the best stories do, of course.

So, Once Upon A Time, and imagine if you can, a steep-sided valley cluttered with giant, spiky green pine trees and thick, green grass that reaches to the top of your socks so that when you run, you have to bring your knees up high, like running through water. Wildflowers spread their sweet heady perfume along the gentle breezes and bees hum musically to themselves as they cheerily collect flower pollen.

People are very happy here and they work hard, keeping their houses spick and span and their children's faces clean.

This particular summer had been very hot and dry, making the lean farm dogs sleepy and still. Farmers whistled lazily to themselves and would stand and stare into the distance, trying to remember what it was that they were supposed to be doing. By two o'clock in the afternoon, the town would be in a haze of slumber, with grandmas nodding off over their knitting and farmers snoozing in the haystacks. It was very, very hot.

The Dragon Rock (commentary)

Although you cannot see the whole story here in this excerpt, the title of the story is indicative of the story's content, which is common in stories for children. There is a dragon that looks like a rock in this story, so the title *The Dragon Rock* is clearly lexically cohesive with the content. The titles of stories for young people, such as *Harry Potter and the Half-Blood Prince*, which features both a boy named Harry and a prince, are often clearly related to their characters. (Almost any Disney film title simply names its main character: *Mulan, Pocahontas, Cinderella…*) Titles for mature audiences, like *Sense and Sensibility* or *The Unbearable Lightness of Being*, are not as directly connected to the contents of those novels.

The mood adjunct *of course* in the first paragraph marks the obviousness of the declarative. The author seems to expect that her audience, children, will be familiar with "Once Upon A Time" as a common genre convention for the opening of stories such as this one.

The excerpt is mostly in declarative mood, which is to be expected in a narrative like this one. The mode is written and the text is one-way, so we do not see questions from the author to the audience. (Note that the characters might ask each other questions in the **dialogue**, but here we are looking at the **narration**.) There is one imperative ("imagine if you can") which the author uses to address the audience directly, perhaps to help the children picture themselves as part of the story. (This often happens in children's stories, but perhaps not much in stories for adults.) This is an indication of the difference between the story as a text and as a discourse. Although the words on the page are the text, the author shows an awareness of what is happening outside the text, that is, in the context, and acknowledges the children through her use of *you* twice and *your socks* and *your knees*. The story is the text, the discourse includes the text and its audience.

The verbs, or more precisely the finites, in the first three paragraphs are realised in the present tense: *begins, spread, are* and so on. These verbs indicate that the processes they represent are habits or states. (Don't forget that the present continuous ("I am walking to work") is used for things that are happening now, while the present simple ("I walk to work") is used for states or habitually occurring actions, although they may not be happening right now.) These first three paragraphs describe the generalities of the story.

In the fourth paragraph the tense switches to past: *had, whistled, was* and so on. This indicates the shift to the specifics of this story. (We tend to tell stories using the past tense.) A further indication of this shift to a specific time is the use of the demonstrative reference *this* in the phrase "this particular summer" in the first clause of the fourth paragraph. *This* is used to point to things or times that are close to us.

"This particular summer" is the unmarked theme of the clause it initiates. It contains a reference to time, which is continued in the marked theme "By two o'clock in the afternoon", which initiates the first clause of the third sentence. The author shows some indication of the temporal organisation of this story with these time themes. (More complex stories, such as the Christopher Nolan film *Memento*, are sometimes told achronologically, using flashbacks, flashforwards and *in media res* beginnings, in which the action begins in the middle of the story.)

These language features, and others that you have found, are all typical of this genre. There is nothing wrong with being typical, of course. The author's adherence to these genre conventions helps the audience, children, follow the narration as it is read to them or as they read it themselves. People are comfortable with what they know, so presenting a story that in some ways resembles other stories will make it easier for children to follow. Fairclough (1992, p. 105) refers to this as **constitutive intertextuality**, meaning that features of other stories shape (or "constitute") our expectations about what linguistic features will appear in this one.

At the hairdressers (Data collected by Bansri Kakkad)

Transcription notations

↗	= rising intonation
[	= overlapping turn, both speakers begin at the same time
——	= stress
<.>	= pause of about one second
<5>	= pause of about five seconds
:	= the sound before the colon is noticeably lengthened
@	= laughter
H	= hairdresser
C	= customer
((trancriber's comment inserted for clarification))	

```
01 H:   [hi:ya
02 C:   [hey: <.> how's it going
03 H:   good thanks <.> how about you
04 C:   yeah good        [thanks
05 H:                    [you want me to take that ((H takes C's coat))
06 C:   <5> cheers <.> it's so nice and warm in here
07 H:   mmm <.> haven't seen you in a while <.> wow <.> your hair's
08      become really long [hasn't it
09 C:                      [yeah <.> I know: <.> sorry <.>
10      [been so busy with uni work and everyfink ((='everything'))
11 H:   [aww:  don't worry
```

```
12 C: <.> but I always say that don't i @
13 H: @ yeah <.> so what we doing today
14 C: um: <.> not too sure <.> [what dyu think
15 H:                          [what about taking it shorter
16 C: well nothing that dramatic maybe just a trim
17 H: uh huh
18 C: <.> I wanna keep my layers [long
19 H:                            [uh huh
20 C: can you show me before doing it
21 H: up to ↗here
22 C: perfect
23 H: okay do you wanna go over to one of the basins
((The conversation continues.))
```

At the hairdressers (commentary)

To explain the purpose of this conversation, it is useful to consider the extract as two separate segments. The first segment, from line 01 to about line 13, is *phatic communication* while the second segment, from lines 13–25, has an *instrumental* purpose. In the first segment the two speakers are renewing their acquaintance, making it clear that they know each other and that they share an ongoing relationship. There is some intersection in the purposes of the conversation in lines 07 and 08. Here *H*'s utterance "your hair's become really long" signals the beginning of a shift from phatic talk to a discussion of hair. If *H* were a friend, we might interpret a comment about hair as purely phatic, but as *H* is a hairdresser, her shift in topic to the field of *hair* seems to be instrumental. Note that after this mention of "hair" other words in the same field begin to appear: "shorter" (line 15), "trim" (line 16), "layers" (line 18) and "basins" (line 23).

Although this is just one conversation between these two people, it exists as part of a discourse that includes the co-text of all their other interactions. The *tenor* of their relationship, which seems to be a friendly one, is signalled from the beginning by overlapping adjacency pair greetings in lines 01 and 02 and further phatic questions and answers in subsequent lines. They've already established a relationship in other interactions; this is acknowledged by *H* in line 07 with "haven't seen you in a while". Other signs of the informal tenor include the use of contractions ("how's" line 02), the use of general high-frequency lexis and the use of ellipsis (omitted *do* before "you want me..." (line 05); omitted *I* before "been so busy..." (line 10).

An additional sign of friendliness can be seen in the way *H* and *C* overlap with each other's utterances several times without seeming to cause irritation. Notice how in line 04, to take one example, *C*'s turn could be finished after the word TCU "good". *H* anticipates the end of *C*'s turn and begins speaking in line 5, not realising that *C* will add "thanks". In a more formal situation we might expect speakers to wait slightly longer before speaking for fear of seeming rude. Here the overlaps are likely seen as collaborative, not as attempts to interrupt, and thus they signal the equality of their relationship. We might expect fewer overlaps in a situation such as a police interview, doctor's appointment or classroom, where one person is more clearly in charge.

Further evidence of equality can be seen by doing a simple quantitative analysis: the speakers take roughly the same number of turns, their turns are all quite short and they speak roughly the same number of words. In some situations we would expect to see quite different patterns in these areas. For example, a lecturer will take lengthy turns between audience turns, as the lecturer has the power to hold the floor.

If we look at the grammatical mood of the clauses used, we see that both speakers use declaratives and interrogatives. Marked use of interrogatives is sometimes a sign of power behind the discourse. A teacher controls student talk by asking numerous questions, as does an interviewer when questioning a job applicant. In this conversation we do not see a preponderance of questions by either speaker. We also do not see the imperative mood. In line 23, *H* wants to direct *C* to move. Instead of being direct by using an imperative clause such as "Go over to one of the basins", *H* is indirect, using the interrogative "do you wanna go over to one of the basins".

As the speakers are together in a hairdressers, they can rely on *situational knowledge* to interpret "what we doing" (line 13) as meaning "what are we doing about your hair" and "here" (line 06) to mean "in this shop". If I had not mentioned that this conversation took place in a hairdressers, you would be uncertain as to its location, though you might guess based on the field-specific lexis mentioned earlier. *H*'s question in line 21 "up to ↗here" is probably accompanied by a hand gesture signalling just where "here" is.

Exophoric references like both these uses of "here" are common in the spoken *mode* as they are interpretable to participants who can see one another.

Although we can't hear this conversation, we can guess at *C*'s London English *variety* from the transcription's inclusion of "everyfink" (line 10) as an approximation of her pronunciation of the word *everything*. (In reality, each word she says is in her accent, but for the reader's convenience only this word has been spelled unconventionally.) *C* is British, more precisely a Londoner, and "everyfink" is a phonological variant common in that city. Of course, *C* may be a Londoner who now lives outside of Britain; our accents are one thing we always take with us when we travel.

Final thoughts

When we use language, we make a series of choices as we write or speak. There is no default best choice of words for any situation. Even a simple spoken greeting involves numerous considerations: Is the context formal or informal?, Is it institutional or social?, Do the speakers know each other or not?, Is one person greeting many people or just one person?, Are the speakers members of a particular speech community with their own idiosyncratic greetings?, and so on. I was once walking with a friend on a city street when he approached another man and said, "Are the fish biting today?" The second man looked surprised for a moment, then laughed and started talking. I started listening, intrigued to hear how that could function as a conversation starter. It seemed that the two had met on a fishing trip once years before. Despite having not met since, the mention of fishing in my friend's greeting was enough to provoke recognition from the other man and to start a conversation. My friend must have made a rapid series of choices before talking: Do I know him? Should I greet him? Should I say "hello" or something unusual? Will he understand "Are the fish biting today?" If I hadn't been privy to the conversation that followed, I would likely have been unable to interpret that unusual conversation-starting utterance. Of course, in many situations we are not able to later listen or ask participants why they said or wrote what they did. In those cases we can make some judgements about what happened by relying on the concepts and tools described in this book. We can look at the discourse that has been produced, then work backwards, thinking about what choices must have been made.

For some people, knowing about language is an end in itself. They are naturally drawn to questions about language use, variation, register and so on. For people like this, and I include myself in this group, the world is a never-ending source of linguistic data to be analysed. Fortunately for us, most people are happy to talk about the language they use, especially when we make it clear that we are not judging their language, but that we are treating them as linguistic informants with valuable insights into the multitude of ways that people can speak or write. Take advantage of a shared knowledge of language to try the following exercises.

1. Take a text that is a few sentences long, then delete as many of signs of lexical cohesion as you can. You should be left with very few content words. Ask someone else to fill in the blanks. (He or she can probably create a coherent text, but it is unlikely to be the same topic as the original.)

2. Choose a text with numerous field-specific terms: an electrician's manual, a biology textbook, a business prospectus, or something else that introduces a variety of words in the same collocational field. Make a list of specialised words from the text. Ask people if they can guess what type of text the words came from, starting by telling them one word, then two, and so on until they can guess. Those with more schematic knowledge will find this easier, but you may be surprised at how few words it takes most people to guess correctly.

3. Record then transcribe a minute or two of a conversation. Ask others to read the transcription, then see if they can guess the social variables (age, gender, ethnicity, class and geographical origin) of the speakers. Ask them to identify which words, phrases or clauses seem to be particularly indicative of a certain type of speaker.

4. Choose a short formal text. Rewrite it to make it informal. Ask someone else to rewrite it to make it formal again. Think about why the resulting text is different from the original. (Or perhaps why it is so similar, although that result is less likely.)

5. Find a transcription of a conversation from a film, or transcribe one yourself. If the conversation is typical of most scripted conversations, it will not look natural. Add discourse markers and other signs of natural speech to the transcription. Ask someone else to identify which features you've added. You might find it difficult to disguise your additions.

For some people language is a tool, but not one that they are particularly interested in studying. For these people, I think the most important thing is to consider the difference between descriptive and prescriptive approaches to language analysis. Linguistic description is fascinating. We can hear how people talk and see how they write, then study the discourse without considering what is right or wrong when compared to standard English. On the other hand, sometimes we should follow prescriptive rules. My daughter recently heard me say "There's two dogs over there." She asked if it shouldn't be "There are two dogs over there" instead. I argued that "There's..." was fine in an informal chat, but admitted that in a planned discourse I would like to avoid such errors. I hope that I have managed to do so in this book.

References

Anderson, R., Reynolds, R., Schallert, D. & Goetz, E. (1977). Frameworks for comprehending discourse. *American Educational Research Journal*. 14 (4): 367–338.

Bartlett, F. (1932). *Remembering*. Cambridge: Cambridge University Press.

Bartlett, T. (2014). *Analysing power in language*. Oxon: Routledge.

Brown, G. & Yule, G. (1983). *Discourse analysis*. Cambridge: Cambridge University Press.

Butt, D., Fahey, R., Feez, S., Spinks, S. & Yallop, C. (2000) *Using functional grammar: An explorer's guide*. 2nd edition. Sydney: NCELTR, Macquarie University.

Cook, G. (2011). Discourse analysis. In J. Simpson (ed.) *The Routledge handbook of applied linguistics*. Abingdon: Routledge.

Coupland, N. & Bishop, H. (2007). Ideologised values for British accents. *Journal of Sociolinguistics*. 11 (1): 74–93.

Crystal, D. (2008). Two thousand million? *English Today*. 24 (1): 3–6.

Cutting, J. (2002). *Pragmatics and discourse*. Abingdon: Routledge.

Danes, F. (1974). Functional sentence perspective and the organization of the text. In F. Danes (ed.) *Papers in functional sentence perspective*. Prague: Academia.

De Beaugrande, R. (1980). *Text, discourse and process: Toward a multidisciplinary science of texts*. Norwood, NJ: Ablex.

De Beaugrande, R. & Dressler, W. (1981). *Introduction to text linguistics*. London: Longman.

Dunbar, R. (2004). Gossip in evolutionary perspective. *Review of General Psychology*. 8 (2): 100–110.

Fairclough, N. (1989). *Language and power*. Harlow: Longman.

Fairclough, N. (1992). *Discourse and social change*. Cambridge: Polity Press.

Fraser, B. (1999). What are discourse markers? *Journal of Pragmatics*. 31: 931–952.

Fuller, J. (2003). Use of the discourse marker 'like' in interviews. *Journal of Sociolinguistics*. 7 (3): 365–377.

Fung, L. & Carter, R. (2007). Discourse markers and spoken English: Native and learner use in pedagogic settings. *Applied Linguistics*. 28 (3): 410–439.

Georgakopoulou, A. & Goutsos, D. (2004). *Discourse analysis: An intro-duction.* Edinburgh: Edinburgh University Press.

Goffman, E. (1959). *The presentation of self in everyday life.* Edinburgh: Anchor Books.

Goffman, E. (1974). *Frame analysis: An essay on the organisation of experience.* New York: Harper & Row.

Grice, P. (1975). Logic and conversation. In P. Cole and J. Morgan (eds.) *Syntax and semantics 3: Speech arts.* New York: Academic Press.

Halliday, M. & Hasan, R. (1976). *Cohesion in English.* Harlow: Longman.

Halliday, M. (1978). *Language as social semiotic.* London: Edward Arnold.

Halliday, M., revised by Matthiessen, C. (2004). *An introduction to functional grammar.* London: Arnold.

Hoey, M. (2001). *Textual interaction.* London: Routledge.

Hughes, G. (1990). What is register? *English Today.* 2 (6): 47–51.

Hughes, A., Trudgill, P. & Watt, D. (2005). *English accents and dialects.* London: Hodder Education.

Jackson, H. & Stockwell, P. (2011). *An introduction to the nature and functions of language.* London: Continuum.

Joos, M. (1967). *The five clocks: A linguistic excursion into the five styles of English usage.* New York: Harcourt, Brace and World.

Kaplan, R. (1966). Cultural thought patterns in intercultural education. *Language Learning.* 16 (1): 1-20.

Labov, W. (2006). *The social stratification of English in New York City.* 2nd edition. Cambridge: Cambridge University Press.

Liddicoat, A. (2007). *An introduction to conversation analysis.* London: Continuum.

Maschler, Y. (1994). Metalanguaging and discourse markers in bilingual conversation. *Language in Society.* 23 (3): 325–366.

McArthur, T. (1998). *The English languages.* Cambridge: Cambridge University Press.

Mehl, M., Vazire, S., Ramirez-Esparza, N., Slatcher, R. & Pennebaker, J. (2007). Are women really more talkative than men? *Science.* 317: 82.

Nettle, D. & Dunbar, R. (1997). Social markers and the evolution of reciprocal exchange. *Current Anthropology.* 38: 93–98.

Ochs, E. (1992). Indexing gender. In A. Duranti & C. Goodwin (eds.) *Rethinking context: Language as an interactive phenomenon.* Cambridge: Cambridge University Press.

Radford, A., *et al.* (2009). *Linguistics: An introduction.* Cambridge: Cambridge University Press.

Reyes, A. (2005). Appropriation of African American slang by Asian American youth. *Journal of Sociolinguistics.* 9 (4): 509–532.

Sacks, H., Schegloff, E. & Jefferson, G. (1974). A simplest systematics for the organization of turn-taking for conversation. *Language*. 50 (4): 696–735.

Schank, R. & Abelson, R. (1977). *Scripts, plans, goals, and understanding: An inquiry into human knowledge structures*. Hillsdale, NJ: Lawrence Erlbaum.

Schiffrin, D. (1987). *Discourse markers*. Cambridge: Cambridge University Press.

Strauss, S. & Feiz, P. (2014). *Discourse analysis: Putting our worlds into words*. London: Routledge.

Stubbs, M. (1983). *Discourse analysis*. Oxford: Blackwell.

Swales, J. (1990). *Genre analysis*. Cambridge: Cambridge University Press.

Swann, J., Deumert, A., Lillis, T. & Mesthrie, R. (2004). *A dictionary of sociolinguistics*. Oxford: Elsevier Science Ltd.

Thornbury, S. (2005). *Beyond the sentence: Introducing discourse analysis*. Oxford: Macmillan.

Thorne, S. (2008). *Mastering advanced English language*. Hampshire: Palgrave Macmillan.

Trudgill, P. (1983). *On dialect: Social and geographical perspectives*. Oxford: Blackwell.

Trudgill, P. (2002). *Sociolinguistic variation and change*. Edinburgh: Edinburgh University Press.

Index